CROSSROADS 3

STUDENT BOOK

Shirley A. Brod
Irene Frankel

with

Earl W. Stevick

and

Spring Institute for International Studies

Oxford University Press

Acknowledgments

Thanks to the reviewers and consultants who helped to shape this book:

Fiona Armstrong, New York City Board of Education, New York, New York

Jeffrey Bright, Albany Park Community Center, Chicago, Illinois

Martha F. Burns, North Hollywood Adult Learning Center, North Hollywood, California

Cliff Meyers, University of Massachusetts, Amherst, Massachusetts

Jack Wigfield, Alemany Campus, City College of San Francisco, San Francisco, California

We'd like to thank Oxford University Press for doing so much to facilitate our long-distance collaboration. We'd also like to thank our editors:

Susan Lanzano for so lovingly nurturing this project; Ellen Lehrburger for guiding us through the process; Ken Mencz for his dedication to *Crossroads* and his unfailing patience and enthusiasm; and Allen Appel for taking care of the details. Thanks, too, to everyone else at Oxford, especially Jim O'Connor.

Thanks to those from whom we've learned so much about teaching ESL and teaching adults: Virginia French Allen, James Asher, Charles Curran, John Fanselow, Caleb Gattegno, Autumn Keltner, Stephen Krashen, Harvey Nadler, Jenny Rardin, Liz Steinberg, and Earl Stevick.

Thanks to Margot Gramer and Jenny Rardin for their unique contributions to this series.

Thanks to Myrna Ann Adkins and Barbara Sample of the Spring Institute for International Studies for making it possible for us to work together, and for supporting us in so many ways.

This book is dedicated to our incredible support team, our husbands, David Martin and Jerry Brod; to Irene's other parents, Royal and Robert Martin, for always being there for her; and to Shirley's sons, Stephen, Eric, and Christopher, who have always helped her see the world through younger eyes.

Contents

	COMPETENCIES	GRAMMAR
UNIT 7 **Finding a Job** Page 73	Begin an interview appropriately. End an interview appropriately. Fill in a job application form. Answer questions about your educational background. Describe your work experience, training, job skills, and job strengths.	verb + infinitive *know how to use, like to use,* etc. vs. modal + base form of verb *can use.* adverbs of manner *carefully, neatly,* etc.
UNIT 8 **On the Job** Page 85	Report specific problems found in completing a task. Briefly explain how to work a simple piece of equipment. Identify which part of instructions you did not understand. Respond to a supervisor's comments about the quality of your work. Read a paycheck stub. Tell someone how to do a routine task, giving step-by-step verbal instructions.	indefinite pronouns *one* and *ones*
UNIT 9 **Recreation** Page 97	Ask and answer questions about weekend plans and recreation. Identify major U.S. holidays. Ask and answer questions about holidays in the U.S. and common ways to celebrate them. Read a weather map. Ask and answer questions about the weather. Answer questions about holidays in your country of origin.	future time with *be* + verb + *ing* superlatives of adjectives with *most*
UNIT 10 **Transportation** Page 109	Read a bus schedule. Find a place by following simple written directions. Use a map to find a place. Ask for information about and find recreational facilities on a map.	past continuous tense possessive pronouns *mine, hers,* etc.
Grammar Summaries Page 121		
Tapescript for Listening Plus Page 124		
Basic Conversations for Progress Checks Page 131		
Useful Irregular Verbs Inside back cover		

To the Teacher

Crossroads

- is a four-level adult series in English as a second language
- integrates a competency-based approach with systematic grammar presentation
- covers the four skills of listening, speaking, reading, and writing
- is for adults and young adults in adult education or continuing education programs, but can also be used in secondary programs
- begins lower and progresses more gradually than other beginning series
- provides an exceptionally complete and flexible array of classwork, homework, and teacher support materials through the Student Book, Teacher's Book, Multilevel Activity and Resource Package, the Workbook, and Cassettes.

Level 3

The **Student Book** has ten units with the following sections:

Getting Started	provides a context for new material
Conversations	new competencies, grammar and vocabulary
Paperwork	realia and document literacy
Reading and Writing	literacy skills
Listening Plus	listening skills
Interactions	information gap
Progress Checks	demonstration of competency

The **Teacher's Book** provides:

- warm-up activities and reproducible charts for each unit
- step-by-step procedures for each exercise
- suggestions for varying and extending the exercises
- answer keys
- ways to teach pronunciation
- cross-cultural and linguistic notes
- reproducible versions of unit opener illustrations
- reproducible Competency Checklists.

The **Multilevel Activity and Resource Package** is reproducible and includes:

- grammar and reading worksheets in two versions, for multilevel classes
- grammar focus, interactive listening, guided writing, and simulations worksheets
- pictures for language experience stories
- a dictionary of words from the Student Book and dictionary skills worksheets
- word cards, games, and game boards
- practical teaching notes.

The **Workbook** is designed for independent study and homework. It contains:

- grammar and reading worksheets in two versions, for multilevel classes
- grammar focus and writing worksheets
- answer key.

Practice conversations and the Listening Plus page exercises are recorded on the **Cassettes.**

Placement

Place students in CROSSROADS 1 if they function minimally or not at all in English.

Place students in CROSSROADS 2 if they are able to function in a very limited way, depending largely on learned phrases.

Place students in CROSSROADS 3 if they have moved beyond a limited range of learned phrases and are beginning to function with some independence and creativity, but still have difficulty communicating, even with someone who is used to dealing with people of limited English proficiency.

Place students in CROSSROADS 4 if they can communicate, although with some difficulty, on familiar topics with native speakers who are not accustomed to dealing with people of limited English proficiency.

CROSSROADS is compatible with the Comprehensive Adult Student Assessment System (CASAS) and the Student Performance Levels (SPL's) recommended by the Mainstream English Language Training (MELT) Project of the U.S. Department of Health and Human Services. SPL's are correlated with scores on the Basic English Skills Test (BEST).

	MELT SPL	BEST Score	CASAS Achievement Score
CROSSROADS 1	I and II	9–28	165–190
CROSSROADS 2	III	29–41	191–196
CROSSROADS 3	IV and V	42–57	197–210
CROSSROADS 4	VI and VII	58–65+	211–224

Placement can also be made according to students' control of grammar. CROSSROADS 1 covers the present tense of *be,* the present continuous tense, and the simple present tense. CROSSROADS 2 covers the past tense of *be* and regular verbs, and the future with *be going to.* CROSSROADS 3 covers the past tense with irregular verbs, the future tense with *will,* and the past progressive tense. CROSSROADS 4 covers the present perfect and present perfect continuous tenses.

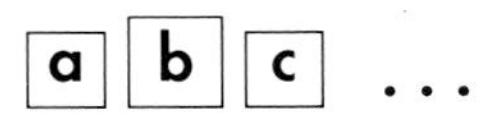

One of these symbols in the margin next to an exercise tells you that a specific competency is first practiced there. In the *Progress Checks* pages, the same letter identifies the exercise that tests that competency.

Teaching Procedures

An underlying principle of CROSSROADS is *elicit before you teach.* We suggest that students guess what the text might say, share any language they already know about the topic, listen to the text on cassette or as read by their teacher, and learn or review key vocabulary. Similarly, before attempting independent pair practice, students might repeat the exercise aloud together, learn needed vocabulary, and participate in supervised pair practice.

Most instruction lines recur throughout the book and stand for, rather than spell out, complete teaching procedures. **Step-by-Step Teaching Procedures** for these recurring exercises appear on pages vii–xi, following this introduction. They state the purpose of the exercise and include preparation and follow-up steps to help students progress at their own pace.

Most exercises are covered by the Step-by-Step Teaching Procedures. Those that are not are covered in the Teacher's Book, which provides an individually tailored procedure for every Student Book exercise.

Many of the exercises in CROSSROADS ask students to provide information about themselves. Most students enjoy this and feel that it helps them learn. However, there may be times when students are unwilling or unable to supply personal information. Therefore, some of the teaching procedures suggest that students may provide fictitious rather than true information.

Progress Checks

The last two pages of each unit are *Progress Checks,* which allow you and the students to find out how well they have mastered the competencies presented in the unit. Even if your program is not competency-based, these exercises provide a useful way for students to demonstrate that they have acquired the language taught in the unit.

Each exercise tests a specific competency or competencies, identified by letter and by name. You can evaluate students yourself, have peers evaluate each other, or have students evaluate themselves. Reproducible Competency Checklists in the back of the Teacher's Book can help with record-keeping.

The two-part exercises called *What are the people saying? / Do it yourself* allow students to demonstrate spoken competencies. In *What are the people saying?,* students work in pairs or alone to generate a conversation based on what they have practiced in the unit. They are prompted by pictures, and some of the words and sentences may be supplied. This first part of the exercise provides a review of what students have practiced, and also lets them demonstrate how well they control the grammatical structures involved. *What are the people saying?* can be done just orally, or followed up with writing. An Answer Key for *What are the people saying?* appears in the back of the Student Book. The second part of the exercise, *Do it yourself,* is where competency is demonstrated.

When a competency requires reading *(Read unit pricing labels, Read bus schedules),* the needed reading material is provided in the exercise. Progress Checks are designed for classroom use, but most competencies are actually needed outside of the classroom, in the community. For this reason, *Do it yourself* sometimes involves a degree of role play and imagination. For example, to demonstrate the competency *Follow directions,* students use a map and point to the place they're directed to.

Culminating Activities

Each unit of Student Book 3 ends with a *Problem Solving* exercise, culminating in a role play. As a group, students identify problems pictured and suggest ways to solve the problem. These activities encourage students to draw upon all of their communicative resources and to exercise their creativity.

Problem Solving is not an evaluation tool like other exercises on the Progress Checks pages. It provides an opportunity for the students to bring their new language skills to bear on a fairly complex and extended task. Success is in completion of the task, rather than in accurate production of language.

Grammar Summary, Tapescript, Useful Irregular Verbs

These three sections, together with the Answer Key for *Progress Checks* mentioned above, are located in the back of the Student Book.

The Grammar Summary presents complete paradigms of grammatical structures practiced in the Student Book, including those highlighted in *Focus on grammar* exercises. The Tapescript for Listening Plus lets you preview exercises and to read them aloud if the Cassette is not available. Useful Irregular Verbs includes 95 of the most frequently used irregular verbs in their base and past tense forms.

Step-by-Step Teaching Procedures
(in order of appearance)

GETTING STARTED
Guess.

Provides a context for the unit.
1. Give students a little time to look at the picture.
2. Have students identify the characters, or identify them yourself.
3. Ask where the characters are.
4. Ask students to guess what the characters are doing.
5. Ask students to guess what the characters are saying. All responses are valid here.
6. Respond to each guess by restating it in acceptable English.

What can you hear?

Prepares students to read the first conversation on the next page.
1. Have students look at the picture while you play the tape or read the conversation aloud.
2. Have students volunteer any words or sentences they can recall from the conversation.
3. Acknowledge all contributions by restating them in acceptable English. Write them on the board.

CONVERSATIONS
Practice. *(the first conversation in the unit)*

Introduces specific competencies, grammar, and/or vocabulary.
1. Have students compare the words, phrases, or sentences on the board (from *What can you hear?*) with the ones in the book.
2. Play the tape or read the conversation aloud while students follow along silently in their books.
3. Use the pictures on the previous page or otherwise elicit or demonstrate the meaning of key words and phrases.
4. Have students repeat the conversation chorally and then practice in pairs.

What can you say?

Introduces vocabulary.
1. Ask students to look at the picture(s) and say any word, phrases, or sentences they can read or guess.
2. As each item is volunteered, write it on the board or overhead projector in a place corresponding to its location in the exercise.
3. Pronounce each item after you write it. Have students point to the item in their books and repeat it.
4. In the same way, add any words students have not volunteered.
5. Have seated volunteers say the items while a student at the board points.
6. Have students work in pairs, one saying an item and the other pointing.
7. Have students copy the items onto a separate piece of paper, practice writing each item several times, and then dictate the items to each other in pairs.

Focus on grammar.

Helps students infer grammatical principles without using grammar terms.
1. Choose a pair of items that contrast *(Where is the book? / Where are the books?)*. Write the pair side by side on the board or overhead projector.
2. Read the two items aloud and have students repeat.
3. Provide another example like the left-hand item *(Where is the chair?)*, write it underneath, and have students repeat.
4. Elicit the corresponding item for the right-hand column *(Where are the chairs?)*, write it, and have students repeat.
5. Point to the next space in the right-hand column and elicit an example to fill it.
6. Elicit the corresponding item for the left-hand column.
7. Have students copy the items on a separate piece of paper.
8. Use the same procedure for the other contrasting pairs in the exercise.

Practice. *(after the first one in the unit)*

Introduces specific competencies, grammar, and/or vocabulary.
1. Play the tape or read the conversation aloud while students follow along silently in their books.
2. Ask students to set the scene, saying who the characters are, where they are, and what they are doing.

3. Elicit or demonstrate the meaning of key words and phrases.
4. Play the tape again and ask questions to check comprehension.
5. Have students repeat the conversation chorally and then practice in pairs.

Talk about ________ .

Provides practice with competencies, grammar, and vocabulary.

1. Read the cues aloud and have students repeat.
2. Read the conversation aloud and have students repeat.
3. Have two volunteers say the conversation for the class, using the first cue.
4. Have students practice the conversation in pairs, changing partners, saying both parts, and using all the cues.

Talk about your________ / yourself.

Provides practice with competencies, grammar, and vocabulary.
Note: In some of these exercises, students may want or need to give fictitious information about themselves. Tell students that this is acceptable.

1. Read the conversation aloud and have students repeat. Then have a volunteer say the conversation with you; provide your personal information where appropriate.
2. Have two volunteers say the conversation for the class, providing their personal information where appropriate.
3. Have students practice the conversation in pairs, using all the cues. Then have them change partners and roles.

PAPERWORK

Read the form/ads/labels, etc.

Introduces vocabulary for these documents.

1. Draw an outline of the form or other document on the board or overhead projector.
2. Have students look at the form in their books and read aloud anything they can.
3. As each item is suggested, add it to the form on the board, say it, and have students repeat. Elicit or supply missing items.
4. Point to items on the form at random and have volunteers read them aloud.
5. Ask simple questions to check and confirm students' understanding of vocabulary. *(What did Alfredo study in school?* or *What was Alfredo's mark in Reading?)*
6. Call on a few volunteers to ask and answer questions like those in Step 5.
7. Have students work in pairs to ask and answer questions like those in Step 5.

Add questions with your classmates. Then interview three classmates.

Lets students exchange personal information.
Note: Students may want or need to give fictitious information about themselves. Tell students that this is acceptable.

1. Copy the questions in columns on the board or overhead projector. Don't fill in the answers yet.
2. Have a student ask you the first question. Give the answer in the example, and write it on the board. Do the same with the other questions.
3. Invite students to contribute a few additional interview questions based on the form/ads/labels, etc. in Exercise 1. Write their questions in columns on the board and have the class correct any errors. Leave the questions on the board for Exercise 4.
4. Say the interview questions one at a time and have students repeat. Have students copy the questions on a separate piece of paper.
5. Have volunteers ask and answer the questions for the class.
6. Have students work in groups of four to ask and answer the questions and to write their answers.

Pool your information. Then write summary sentences.

Provides collaborative practice in collecting and summarizing information.

1. Have each group from Exercise 3 choose a secretary. Using the questions from Exercise 3, have each secretary write his group's answers (including his own) in the correct columns on the board.
2. Direct the class to tally the information (e.g., 8–Spanish, 6–Vietnamese, 3–Khmer, 2–Russian, and 1–Korean).
3. Model the first summary sentence (e.g., *Eight students speak Spanish as a first language, six students speak Vietnamese, etc.*).
4. Repeat the process with the other questions, letting students volunteer the summary statements. Have the class correct any mistakes.
5. Have students copy the summary statements in paragraph form.

READING AND WRITING

What can you say about ________ ?

Prepares students for the reading which follows.

1. Have students look at the illustration(s) or form and say anything they can about it/them. If students use or ask about important words in the reading, write them on the board. Say the words and have students repeat.
2. Elicit or explain meanings of words on the board or other key words in the illustrations.
3. Point to the words on the board at random and have students read them aloud.

Read _______ . / Read about _______ . Circle a word you want to learn. Work with your classmates. Find out what it means.

Provides practice in reading connected discourse. Provides a cooperative process for learning new vocabulary.

1. Have students read the text silently and circle the one word they most want to learn.
2. Call on students to say (or spell) their circled words. Pronounce them and write them on the board or overhead projector.
3. Ask if anyone can explain what any of the words mean. Encourage students to contribute until everyone understands the meanings. Allow students to use dictionaries. Supply explanations yourself as a last resort.
4. Continue the process until all circled words have been explained.
5. Ask volunteers to read the narrative aloud.
6. Ask questions to check comprehension.

Read your _______ to your group.

Lets students share their writing.

1. Have a volunteer read her writing aloud to the class. Lead the class in applause for the reader.
2. Have the class restate the writing to confirm understanding. Have the volunteer clarify meaning, if necessary.
3. Have students work in groups to read their writing in turn and to receive applause and responses from their peers.
4. Have students copy their writing on a separate piece of paper.
5. "Publish" the writings by posting them in the classroom.

What has surprised you about _______ in the U.S.? Write about it.

Provides an opportunity for free writing without correction.

1. Read the question aloud.
2. Have students discuss the topic in pairs. Ask a few students to share their ideas with the whole class.
3. Have students write about the topic for a limited time (or have students write at home).
4. To encourage students to write more fluently, don't correct the writing. Instead, respond only to content.

LISTENING PLUS

Notice the difference. Point. Listen and write the sentences.

Helps students become aware of reductions and elisions in speech.

Note: Students are expected to recognize the reductions and elisions, but not produce them.

Notice the difference.

1. Play the instructions on the tape or read them aloud from the tapescript. Check that students understand what to do.
2. Write the words on the left on the board or overhead projector. Tell the students that these are the words we *read.*
3. Write the reduced forms on the right on the board or overhead projector, pronounce them, and tell students that this is what we *hear.*
4. Play the tape or read the examples from the tapescript aloud so that students can clearly hear the difference.
5. Have students give you a few examples of sentences with the words on the left, and write them on the board.
6. Say the first sentence on the board, pronouncing each word clearly. Then say it at normal speed, to illustrate the reduction/elision. Let students know that they will usually hear reduced forms in natural speech. Repeat the process with the other sentences from the board.

Point.

1. Play the instructions on the tape or read them aloud from the tapescript. Check that students understand what to do.
2. Play the tape or read the first sentence in the tapescript aloud. Point to the reduced form on the board as students hear it.
3. Play the rest of the sentences one by one. Have one student go to the board to point while the other students point in their books.

Listen and write the sentences.

1. Play the instructions on the tape or read them aloud from the tapescript. Check that students understand what to do.
2. Play the tape or read one sentence at a time. Have students write the sentences in their books.
3. Have volunteers write the sentences on the board. Have the other students correct any errors.
4. Let students hear the items once again to verify their answers.

Point. Write./Number./Check./Circle.

Gives practice in focused listening.
Note: In this exercise, students will hear short conversations beyond the level they are expected to produce or even completely understand.

Point.

1. Play the instructions on the tape or read them aloud from the tapescript. Check that students understand what to do.
2. Play the tape or read the conversations or narratives one at a time. Have students listen and point in their books.
3. Draw a rough sketch of the pictures on the board, and have a student go to the board. Play the tape or read the tapescript aloud, having the student at the board point to the appropriate picture on the board while the other students point in their books.

Write.

1. Play the instructions on the tape or read them aloud from the tapescript. Check that students understand what to do.
2. Have students close their books. Play the tape or read the first conversation aloud from the tapescript.
3. Have students think of possible answers. Play the first conversation as many times as needed. Have students volunteer their answers. Write their suggestions on the board or overhead projector, and let students discuss them.
4. Have students open their books and compare their answers with the handwritten example in the text.
5. Play the other conversation(s). Have a volunteer work at the board while other students work alone or in pairs, writing their answers.
6. Let students discuss their answers, then play the tape once more so that students can verify their answers.

Number. / Check. / Circle.

1. Play the instructions on the tape or read them aloud from the tapescript. Check that students understand what to do.
2. Play the tape or read the tapescript aloud, one conversation at a time, as many times as students need. Have students number the illustrations in the order of the conversations they hear, or check or circle the items in the illustration or chart.
3. Have students compare their answers in pairs.
4. Play the tape again and have a volunteer write the answers on the board. Correct any errors with the whole class.

What about you?

Gives practice in listening to and responding with personal information.

1. Play the tape or read the tapescript as many times as students need.
2. Have students answer the question by writing similar information about themselves. Circulate to give help and feedback.
3. Have several volunteers put their answers on the board. Correct any errors with the whole class.
4. Have students compare their own answers with the answers on the board, then check each other's answers in pairs.

INTERACTIONS

Get information. / Give information.

Provides an information gap for communicative practice of grammar and vocabulary.

1. Write the conversation on the board or overhead projector. Don't fill in the handwritten parts yet.
2. Review vocabulary students will be using in the exercise.
3. Show students that there are two pages. Divide the class into a Student A group and a Student B group. Have them each open their books to the appropriate page.
4. Show students where A and B get their information and where to write their answers.
5. In the conversation on the board, fill in the blanks as in the example and read the conversation aloud.
6. Call on a volunteer from each group to say the conversation for the class.
7. Erase the information in the blanks. Call on other volunteers to say the conversation using the next cue. Fill in the blanks.
8. Have A's work with B's in pairs to do the exercises and fill in the information. Then have them compare their pages, which should be the same. Each student should change roles and do both pages.

PROGRESS CHECKS

What are the people saying?/Do it yourself.

Provides for demonstration of competency.

What are the people saying?

1. Have students work in pairs to identify the situation, the relationship of the people, and what the people are saying. Circulate to give help and feedback.
2. Have students generate the conversation in the bubbles, either individually or with partners, orally or in writing.
3. Have students work in two-pair groups to compare their answers and conversations.
4. Have a pair or group of volunteers act out the conversation for the class. Have the other students approve what they say or suggest changes.

Do it yourself.

1. Have students say both parts of the conversation with a partner, using their own information and/or whatever cues are supplied.
2. When a student has successfully demonstrated a competency, it can be checked off and dated or initialed.

PROBLEM-SOLVING

What's ________ 's problem?
What should ________ do?

Lets students apply their experience to group problem-solving activities.

What's ________ 's problem?

1. Have students work in pairs or small groups for a few minutes to describe the problem in the illustration. Prompt students by asking questions about the person or people in the illustration.
2. Call on volunteers to speak for their groups. Write all suggestions on the board or overhead projector.
3. Have the class discuss which statements best describe the problem.

What should ________ do?

1. Have the students return to their groups to discuss what the character(s) should do. Groups may come up with more than one solution.
2. Call on volunteers to speak for their groups. Write all suggestions on the board or overhead projector.
3. Have the class discuss which solutions they like best, giving reasons for their choices. Some solutions may be culturally inappropriate in the U.S. Explain why.

Now role play.

Provides an opportunity for creative language use.

1. Have volunteers take the parts of the characters. If the class is large, you may want to use several casts of characters.
2. Have them "perform" the whole story with one of the suggested solutions.
3. Lead the other students in applause.
4. Have students discuss the outcome. Was the problem solved?

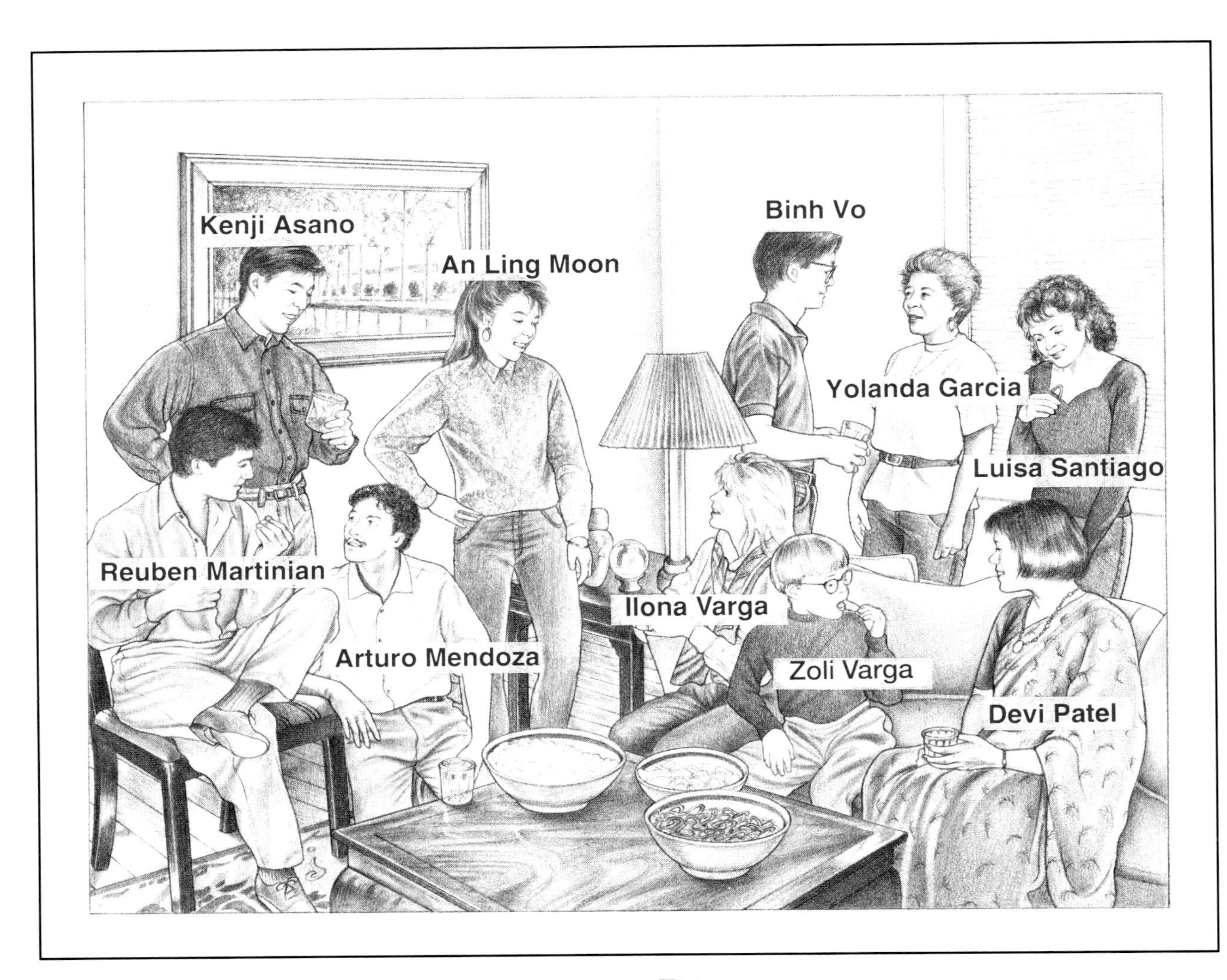

The Class Party

UNIT 1 Introductions

Getting Started

1. Guess. Where are Luisa, Devi, and Binh? What are they doing? What are they saying?

2. What can you hear?

Conversations

1. Practice.

Luisa: Hi, Devi. It's good to see you.
Devi: Hi, Luisa. How are you doing?
Luisa: Fine, thanks. Devi, this is Binh Vo. Binh, this is Devi Patel. Binh was in my class at Westside last year.
Devi: Glad to meet you, Binh.
Binh: Nice to meet you, too.

2. Introduce two classmates.

A: Hi, ______________.

B: Hi, ______________. How are you doing?

A: Fine, thanks. ______________, this is ______________ ______________.

______________, this is ______________ ______________.

B: ______________ to meet you, ______________.

C: ______________ to meet you, too.

3. Practice.

Devi: Where are you from, Binh?
Binh: I'm from Vietnam. What about you?
Devi: I'm from India.
Binh: Were you at Westside last year?
Devi: Yes, I was. I was in the 7:00 class.

4. Focus on grammar. Review.

Was	she	a student? happy?
Were	they / you	students? happy?

Yes, she was.
No, she wasn't.
Yes, they were.
No, they weren't.

Where	was	he	yesterday? last Tuesday?
When	were	they / you	in Mexico? in New York?

He	wasn't / was	at home. in school.	
They / We	were / weren't	there	in May. in 1991.

Conversations

5. Talk about the students.

A: Where is Reuben from?

B: He's from Armenia.

A: Was he at Westside last year?

B: No, he wasn't.

He was in Chicago last year.

Reuben
Armenia
in Chicago

Ilona
Hungary
the morning class

Arturo and Luisa
Mexico
the 6:30 class

An Ling
Korea
in Korea

C

6. Talk about yourself.

A: Where are you from, ______________?

B: I'm from ______________.

A: Were you a student here last year?

B: Yes, I was. I was in ______________ class.

OR

No, I wasn't. I was ______________ last year.

What about you?

A: ______________________________.

Conversations

7. Introduce your partner to the class.

8. Practice.

Binh: It was nice to meet you, Devi.
Devi: Same here.
And it was good to see you again, Luisa.
Binh: Thanks for the great party.
Luisa: Thanks for coming. See you soon.
Binh: Goodbye.
Devi: So long.

d

9. Say goodbye to your partner.

A: It was nice to meet you.

B: Same here.

A: Goodbye.

B: ____________________.

Paperwork

1. Read the personal information form.

WESTSIDE COMMUNITY ADULT SCHOOL

PERSONAL INFORMATION FORM

Name:

Mr./Mrs./Miss/Ms. ______________________________
Last First Middle

Mailing Address: ______________________________

____
City State ZIP

Phone: (______) ______________________________

Social Security No.: ______________________________

Age: __________ Sex: __________ Date of Birth: __________

Marital Status: __________ Maiden Name: __________

Place of Birth: __________ First Language: __________

______________________________ ______________________________
Signature Date

e **2. Fill in the form.**

3. Add questions with your classmates. Then interview three classmates.

What's your first language? Spanish

What's your marital status? single

What's your place of birth? Mexico

______________________________?

4. Pool your information. Then write summary sentences. (For example, *Ten students speak Spanish.*)

Reading and Writing

1. What can you say about Binh's arrival in the United States?

2. Read Binh's story.

Binh Vo came to the United States in 1986. His plane landed in San Francisco late at night. Binh was tired because his trip was long. He was alone and he was nervous because he didn't know anyone in California.

Then he saw an American family. First they looked at a picture. Then they looked at Binh and smiled. They said, "Mr. Vo! Binh Vo!" Binh smiled, too. He felt happy because now he wasn't alone.

3. Work in pairs. Answer these questions.

a. Why was Binh tired?

Binh was tired because ______________________________

b. Why was he nervous?

____

c. Why was he happy?

____

4. Tell Binh's story in your own words.

Reading and Writing

5. **Read Luisa's journal.**

My children and I came to Bridgeton last year. We came to live with my brother, Arturo. At the airport, we were worried because Arturo was not there. We waited for a long time. At last, we saw Arturo running through the airport. We were excited to see him. We were surprised because he had balloons for the children and flowers for me. We all felt very happy because we were together.

6. **Work in pairs. How did Luisa feel? Circle the words in her journal, and make a list of the words. Add other words you know that describe feelings.**

worried	________	________
________	________	________
________	________	________

f

7. **Talk to your partner about your arrival in the United States. What did you do? How did you feel? Why? Use the words in 6.**

8. **What surprised you about your arrival in the United States? Write about it.**

Listening Plus

1. Notice the difference.
Point.
Listen and write the sentences.

You see...	***but you hear...***
Was he...?	*Wuh zee...?*
Was she...?	*Wush she...?*

a. ______________________________

b. ______________________________

2. Point.

Write.

a. nervous b. ____________ c. ____________

3. Fill in the information.

	Last Name	***Date of Birth***	***Social Security No.***
An Ling	Moon		
Ilona			
Reuben			

4. What about you?

____

Interactions

Student A

1. Get information. Ask B the numbers. Fill in the blanks.

A: What's number __1__?

B: __D__.

A: Excuse me?

B: __D__ as in __door__.

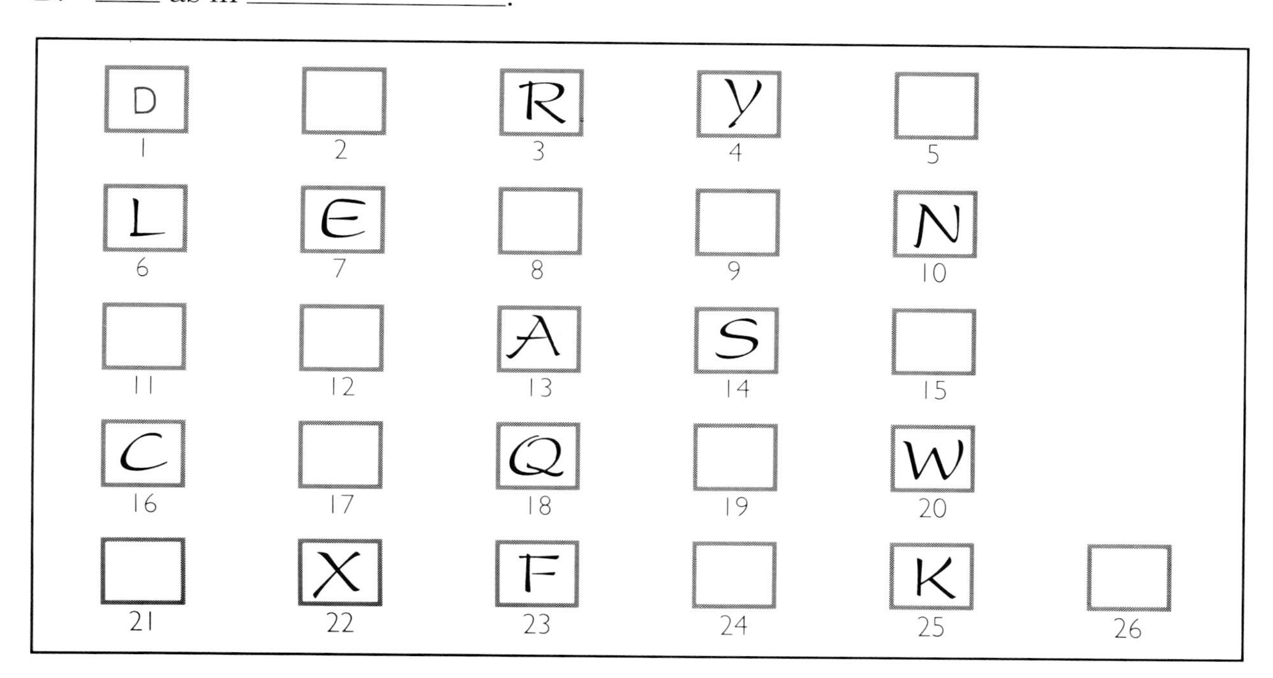

2. Give information. Tell B the numbers.

3. Work with a partner. What's the message?

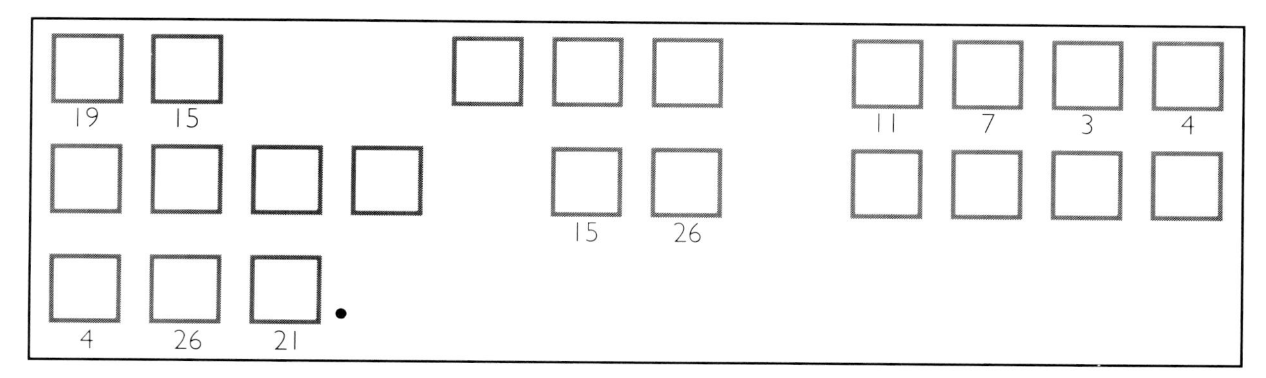

4. Find out about introductions in your partner's country.

Interactions

Student B

1. Give information. Tell A the numbers.

A: What's number 1?

B: D.

A: Excuse me?

B: D as in door.

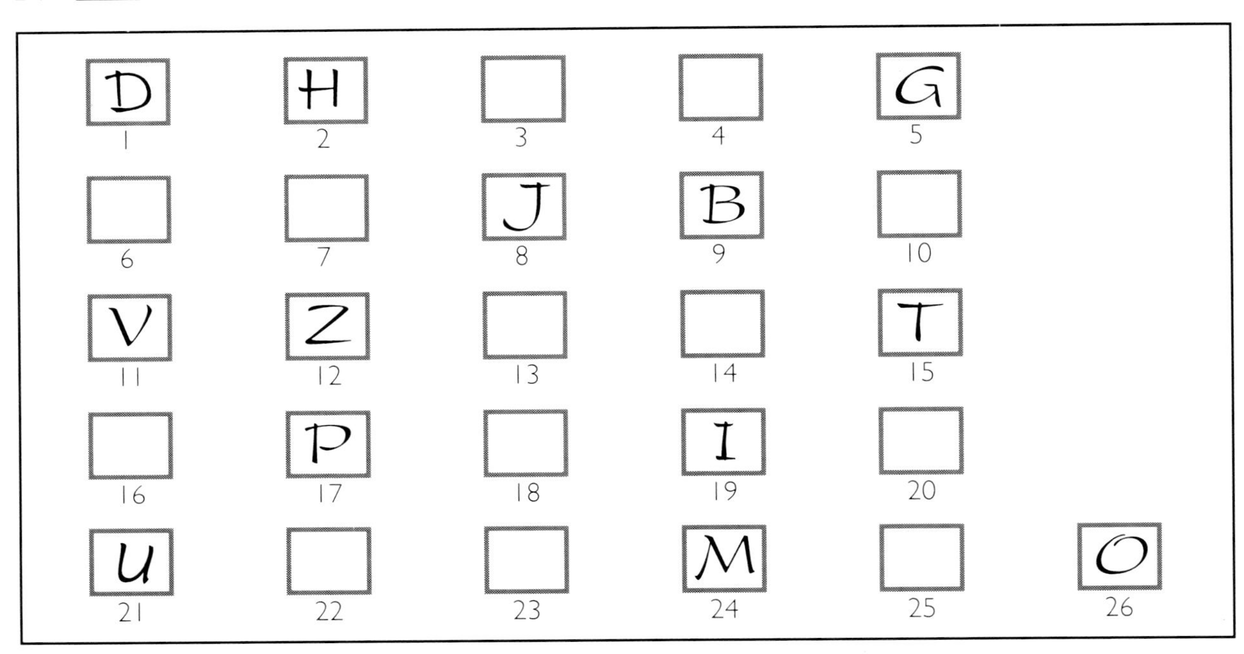

2. Get information. Ask A the numbers. Fill in the blanks.

3. Work with a partner. What's the message?

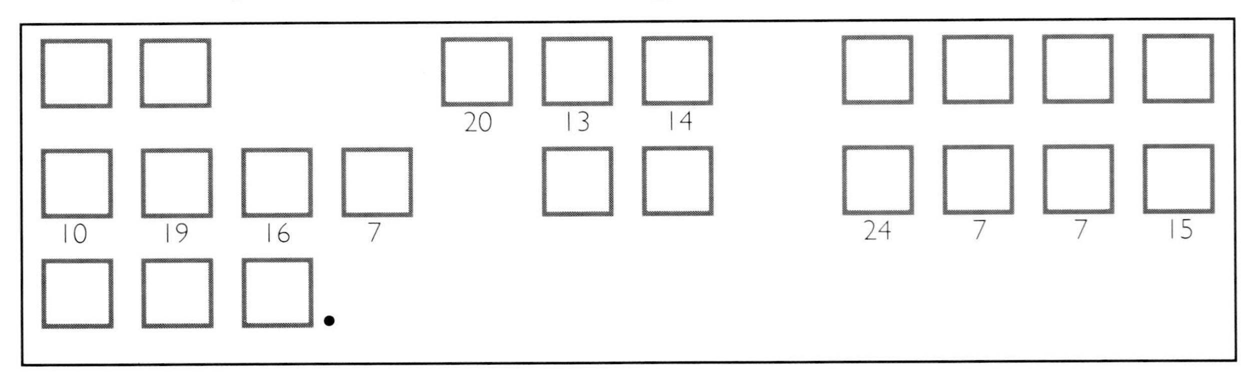

4. Find out about introductions in your partner's country.

Progress Checks

1. **e** ☐ Fill in a personal information form, including middle and maiden names.

Fill in the form.

REGISTRATION FORM

NAME
Mr./Mrs./Miss/Ms. ______________________________
First Middle Last

HOME ADDRESS
____
____
City State ZIP Code

SOC. SEC. NO. _____ – _____ – _____ TELEPHONE (____) ______________

DATE OF BIRTH ______________ MAIDEN NAME ______________

______________ ______________
Date Signature

2. **a** ☐ Say hello.
b ☐ Introduce other people.
d ☐ Say goodbye.

What are the people saying?

Do it yourself.

Progress Checks

3. c ☐ Ask and answer questions about personal backgrounds.
   f ☐ Tell how you felt when you arrived in the United States. Tell why.

What are the people saying?

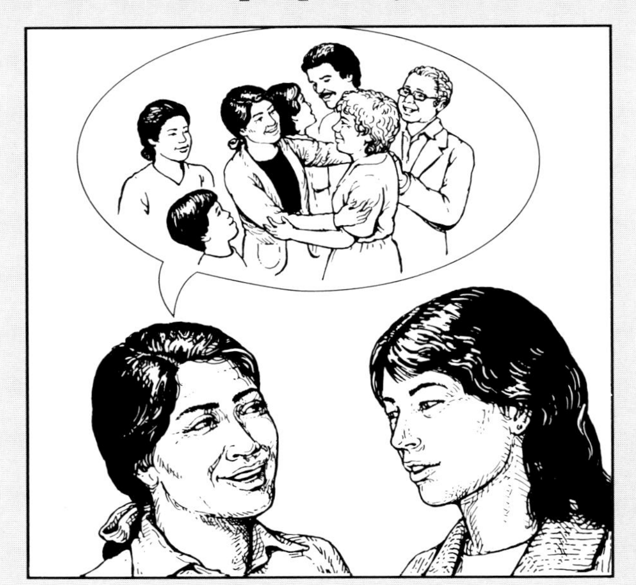

Do it yourself.

Problem Solving

What's Rick's problem?

What can Rick say?
Now role play.

UNIT
2 School

Getting Started

1. **Guess. Where are Luisa and An Ling? What are they doing? What are they saying?**

2. **What can you hear?**

Conversations

1. Practice.

Luisa: Did you get the notice from Chu Son's school?
An Ling: What notice?
Luisa: The notice about parent-teacher conferences.
An Ling: No, I didn't. What does it say?
Luisa: It says, "Parent-Teacher Conferences are on Tuesday, October 18, from 7:00 to 10:00."
An Ling: Thanks, Luisa. I want to talk to Chu Son's teacher. I didn't go to the parent-teacher conference last year.

2. Focus on grammar. Review.

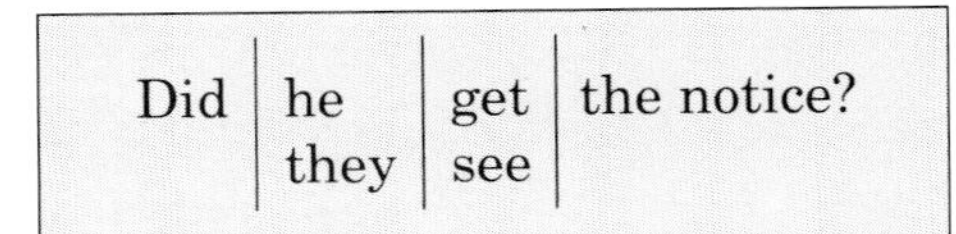

Did	he they	get see	the notice?

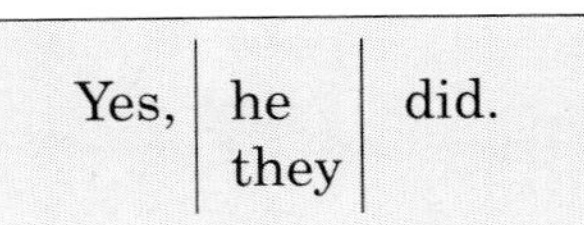

Yes,	he they	did.

No,	he they	didn't.

When Where	did you go to school?

I		talked	to her yesterday.
	didn't	talk	

3. Talk about the school notices.

A: Did you get the notice from school?

B: No, I didn't. What does it say?

A: ______________________________

NOTICE!

Parent-Teacher Conferences on Tuesday, October 18 from 7:00 to 10:00 p.m.

NOTICE

School will close at 1:00 p.m. on Wednesday, November 23.

Happy Thanksgiving!

Notice

Adult School classes will begin on February 5. Call (209) 684-1500 for information.

REGISTER NOW!

Conversations

4. What can you say?

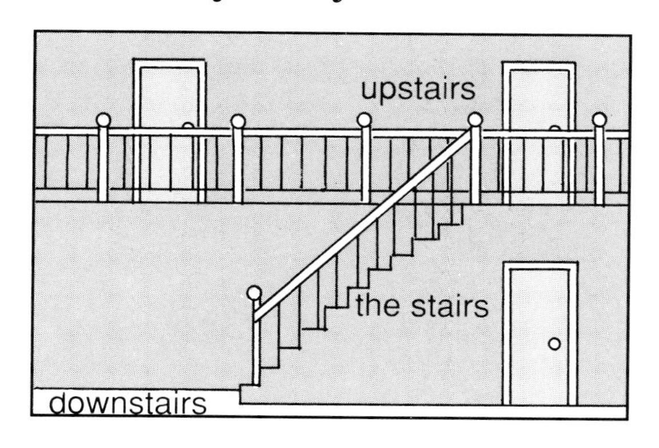

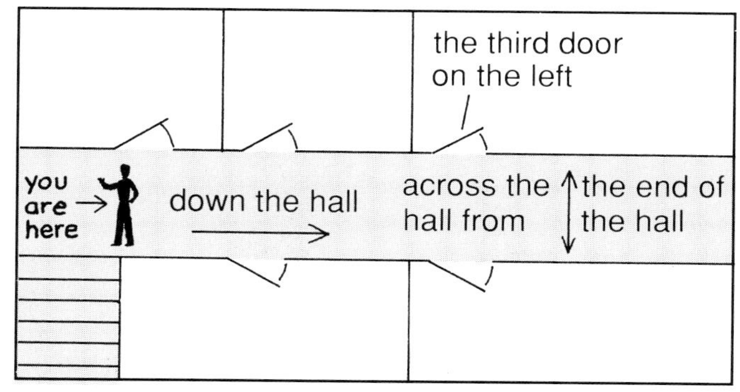

5. Practice.

An Ling: Excuse me. Which way is Room 202?
Custodian: Hmmm. Take the stairs to the second floor.
Turn right and go down the hall.
It's the third door on the left.
It's across from the teacher's room.
An Ling: Go upstairs, turn right,
the third door on the...?
Custodian: On the left.
An Ling: Thanks.

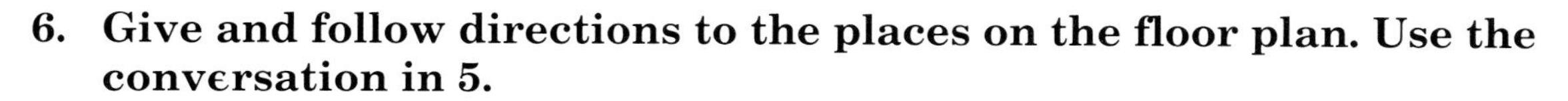

6. Give and follow directions to the places on the floor plan. Use the conversation in 5.

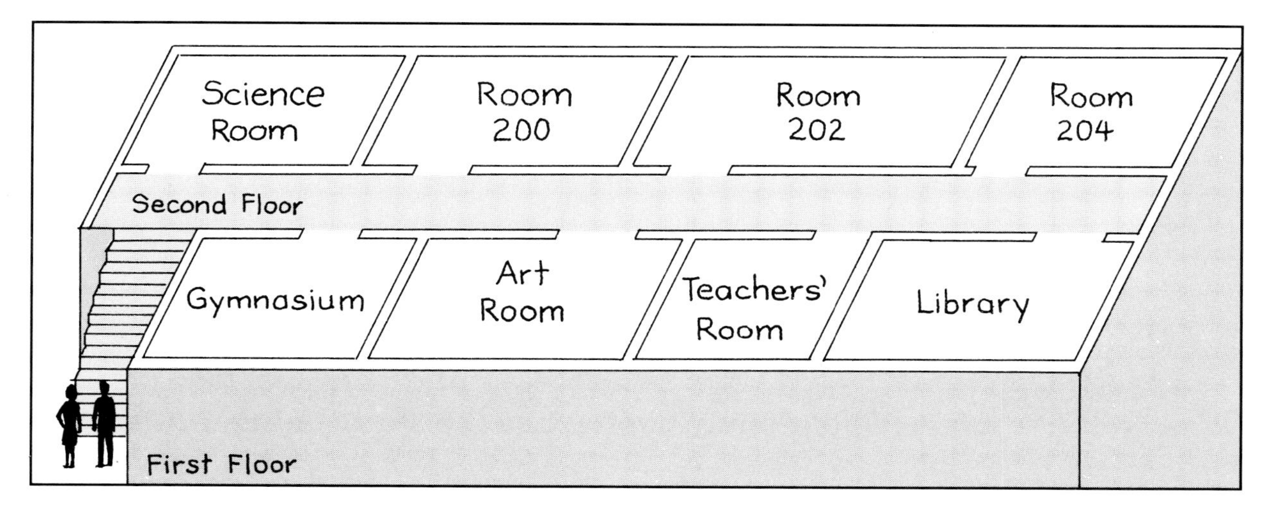

7. Draw a floor plan of your school. Give and follow directions to two places on it.

Conversations

8. Practice.

An Ling: Mrs. Carr, Chu Son is sick a lot and he misses a lot of school. I'm worried about his school work.
Mrs. Carr: Yes. He missed two tests last week.
An Ling: What should he do? Can he take them next week?
Mrs. Carr: Yes, but first he should do the exercises on page 56 in the math book. And he should study the words on page 39 in his spelling book.
An Ling: OK. Thank you very much, Mrs. Carr.

9. Focus on grammar.

Should	he they	study?

Yes,	he they	should.

No,	he they	shouldn't.

What	should	I she	do?

You She	should shouldn't	take the test. study every day.

10. What can you say? Add other good study habits.

GOOD STUDY HABITS

1. Do your homework at the same time every day.
2. Don't watch TV when you study.
3. Don't lie down when you study.
4. Study in a quiet place.
5. Don't study late at night.
6. Work in a well-lit place.

d **11. Give advice about study habits. Use the study habits in 10.**

A: What should I do?

B: You should do your homework at the same time every day.

You shouldn't study late at night.

Paperwork

1. Read Alfredo's report card.

WESTSIDE ELEMENTARY SCHOOL

GRADE 2

Name: Alfredo Santiago — Marking Period: 1st

Days Present: 37 — Days Absent: 8

SUBJECTS		BEHAVIOR	
Reading	C	Participation	U
Math	A	Cooperation	S

A=Excellent B=Good C=Fair D=Poor F=Failing S=Satisfactory U=Unsatisfactory

COMMENTS Alfredo works well with other children, but he's very shy. He needs to speak up in class. He's excellent in math, but he needs help at home with reading.

Teacher's Signature Dorothy Carr

_______________ Date

_______________ Signature of Parent or Guardian

e **2. Match.**

U	Satisfactory
S	Fair
A	Unsatisfactory
C	Excellent

3. Add questions with your classmates. Then interview three classmates.

What did you study in school? math, reading, history, science, and English

What did you like to study in school? math

Did you get a report card? yes

_______________?

4. Pool your information. Then write summary sentences. (For example, *Twelve students got a report card.*)

Reading and Writing

1. What can you say about Zoli Varga?

two weeks ago

last week

today

2. Read Mrs. Smith's note to Ilona and Antal Varga. Circle a word you want to learn. Work with your classmates. Find out what it means.

May 16, 1994

Dear Mr. and Mrs. Varga,

I'm worried about Zoli. He is usually a happy child and a very good student.

Last week, Zoli was very quiet, and he didn't play with his friends. He also didn't participate in class or answer questions. Today, he didn't eat his lunch, and he looked very sleepy.

I would like to talk to you about Zoli. Please call me tomorrow between 1:00 and 2:00 to make an appointment.

Sincerely,
Susan Smith

3. Work in pairs. Answer these questions. Describe Zoli.

1. How does Zoli usually behave? He is usually ____________
2. How did Zoli behave last week? ____________
3. How did Zoli behave today? ____________
4. Guess. What's the matter with Zoli? ____________

Reading and Writing

4. **What can you say about the excuses? Add other good and bad excuses.**

She's sick.

He missed the bus.

There are snow flurries.

5. **Read An Ling's absence note for Chu Son.**

October 31, 1994

Dear Mrs. Carr,

Please excuse Chu Son's absence from school on Thursday and Friday, October 27 and 28. He had a cold and fever, and he had to stay in bed.

Can Chu Son make up his homework? Please send his assignments.

Thank you.

Sincerely,
An Ling Moon

f

6. **Write an absence note for a child or yourself. Use one of the good excuses in 4.**

7. **Read your absence note to your group.**

8. **What has surprised you about attending adult school in the U.S.? Write about it.**

Listening Plus

1. Notice the difference.
Point.
Listen and write the sentences.

You see...	***but you hear...***
Did you...?	*Dih ja...?*
Did he...?	*Dih dee...?*

a. ______________________________

b. ______________________________

2. Point.

Write.

She should study at the kitchen table. ______________________________

3. Fill in the information.

	Day	***Date***	***Time***
First Notice	Tuesday		
Second Notice			
Third Notice			

4. What about you?

____

Interactions
Student A

1. Get directions. Ask B for directions to these places. Label them.

Room 110 Room 106 the library the teacher's room the ladies' room the gym

A: Excuse me. Which way is Room 110?
B: Turn right, go down the hall, and turn left. It's the first door on the left.
A: Turn right, go down the hall, and turn left. First door on the left. Thanks.

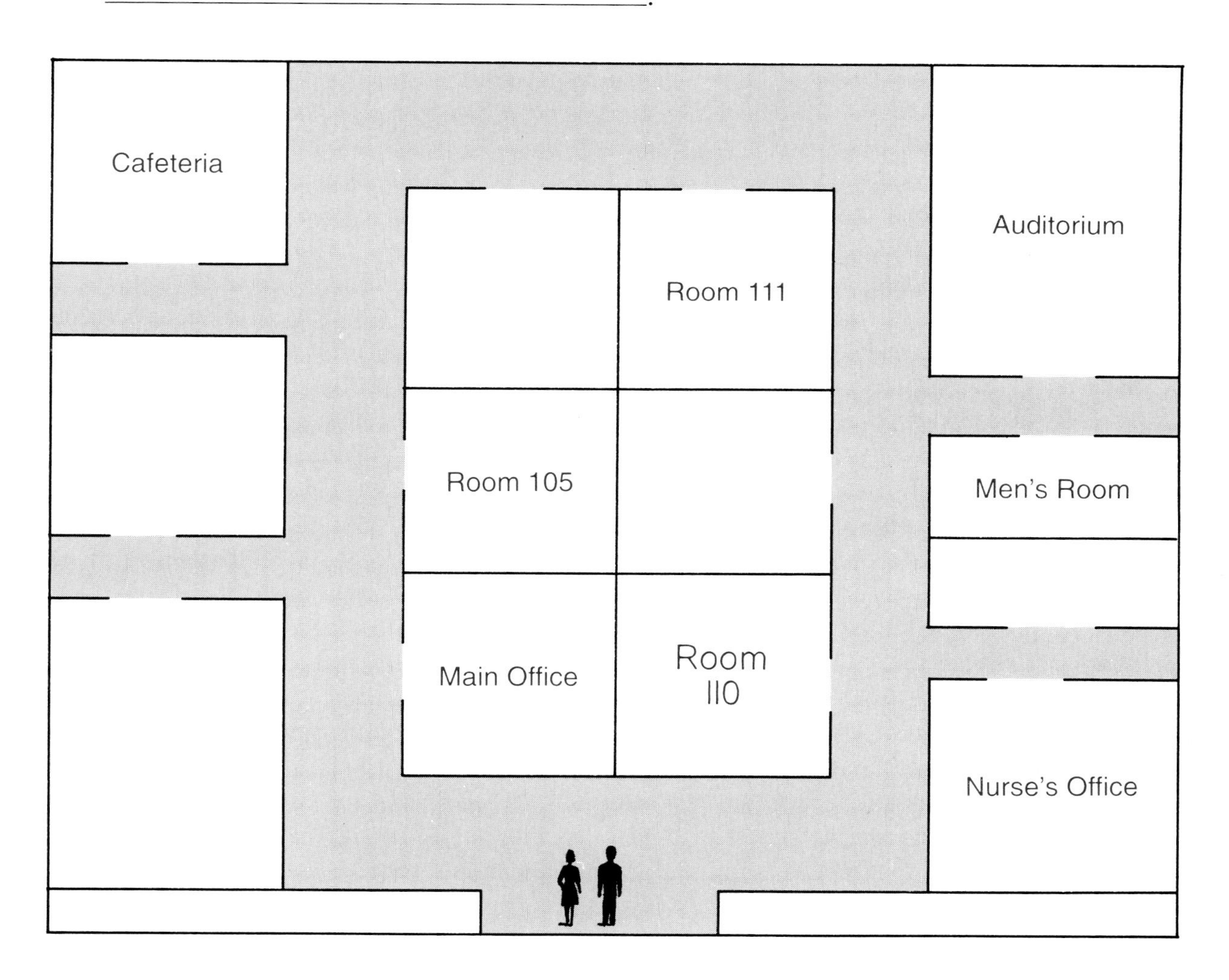

2. Give directions.

3. Find out about school buildings in your partner's country.

Interactions
Student B

1. Give directions.

A: Excuse me. Which way is Room 110?

B: Turn right, go down the hall, and turn left. It's the first door on the left.

A: Turn right, go down the hall, and turn left. First door on the left. Thanks.

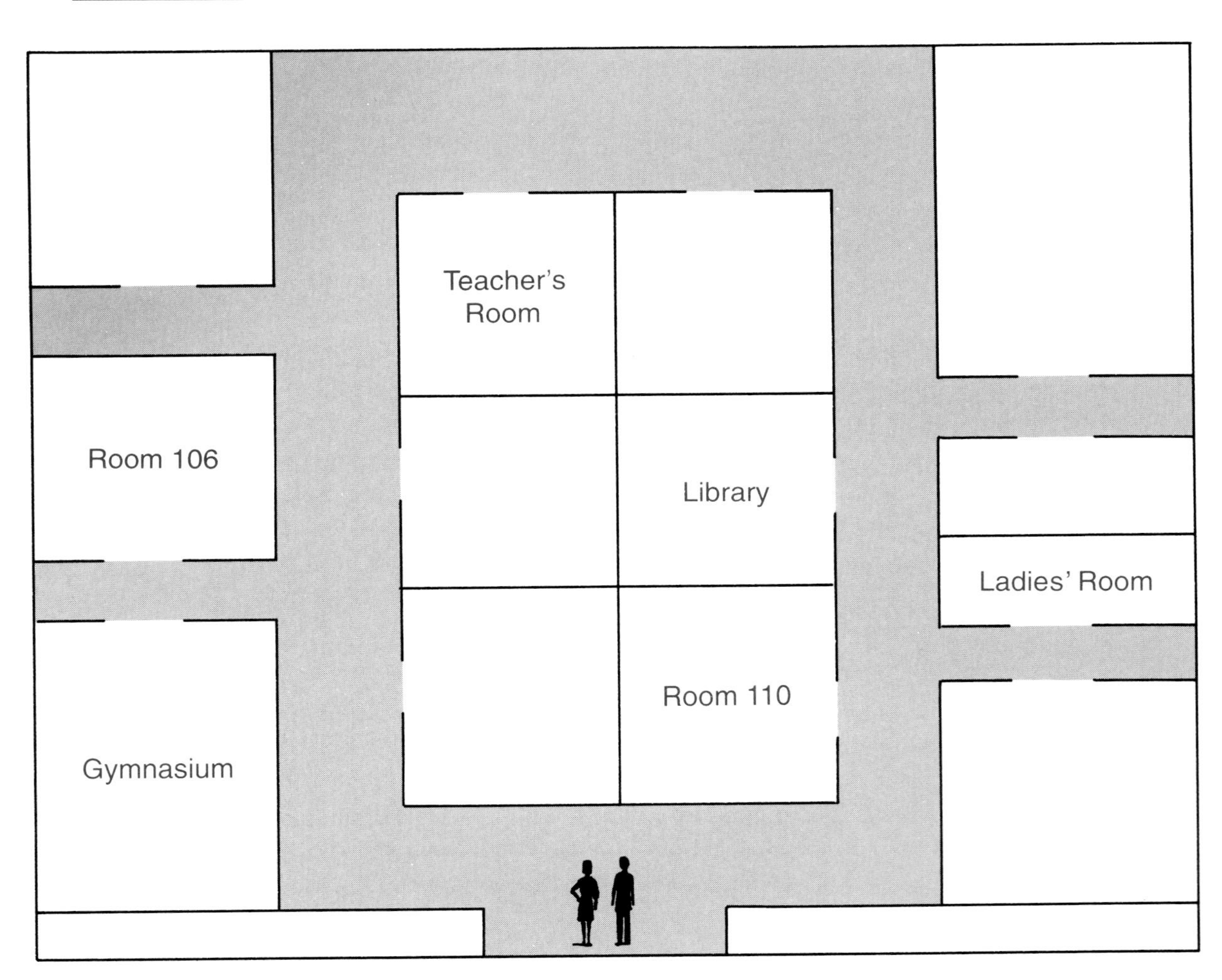

2. Get directions. Ask A for directions to these places. Label them.

the cafeteria the main office Room 111 the nurse's office the auditorium Room 105

3. Find out about school in your partner's country.

Progress Checks

1. **a** ☐ Read notices from a school.

Read the notice and answer the questions.

Westside Community Adult School

End-of-Year Party

Thursday, December 14,
7:00–8:30 p.m.,
in the cafeteria

Donna Jones, Teacher

a. What are the day and date of the party? ____________________

b. Where is the party going to be? ____________________

c. Who is the teacher? ____________________

d. When does the party start? ____________________

2. **e** ☐ Read basic information on a report card.

Read Ben's report card and circle Yes or No.

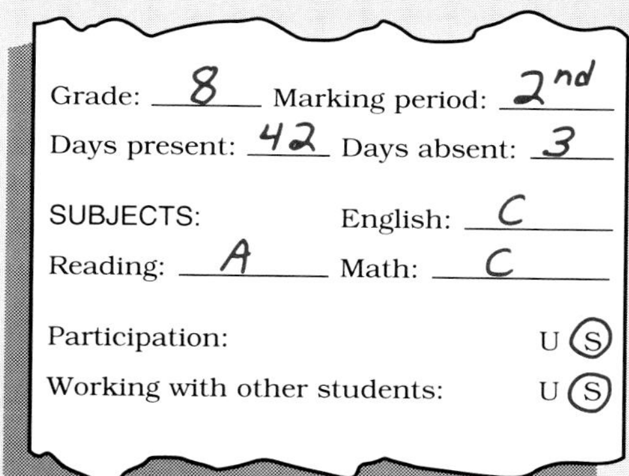
Grade: 8 Marking period: 2nd
Days present: 42 Days absent: 3
SUBJECTS: English: C
Reading: A Math: C
Participation: U (S)
Working with other students: U (S)

a. Ben got a good mark in reading.
Yes No

b. Ben missed 2 days of school.
Yes No

c. Ben got a bad mark in working with other children.
Yes No

d. Ben is in the 2nd grade.
Yes No

3. **b** ☐ Give directions to a specific place in a building.
c ☐ Follow directions to a specific place in a building.

What are the people saying?

Do it yourself.

Progress Checks

4. **f** ☐ Write a note to explain an absence from school or work.

Write a note to your teacher to explain your absence from school. Use real or imaginary information.

5. **d** ☐ Ask for and give advice about study habits.

What are the people saying?

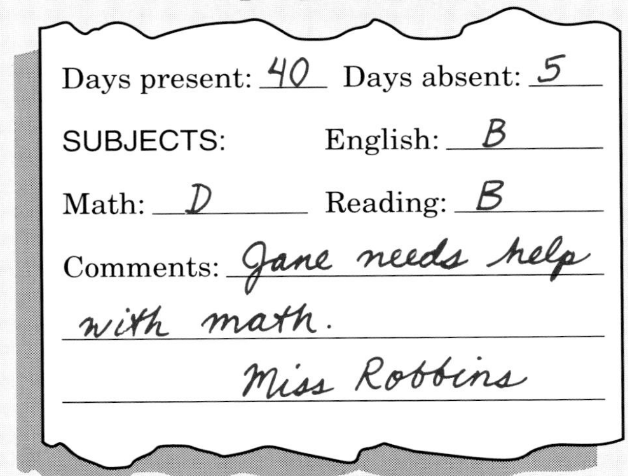

Do it yourself.

Problem Solving

What's Zoli's problem?

What should Zoli do? What should Zoli's parents do?
Now role play.

UNIT

3 The Telephone

Getting Started

1. **Guess. Where are Reuben and Ms. Gaines? What are they doing? What are they saying?**

2. **What can you hear?**

Conversations

1. Practice.

Ms. Gaines: Hello.
Reuben: Hello. This is Reuben Martinian.
I need to see Dr. Brenner. I have a very bad toothache.
Ms. Gaines: Excuse me. I think you have the wrong number.
Reuben: Oh. Is this 667-0987?
Ms. Gaines: No, it isn't.
Reuben: I'm sorry.
Ms. Gaines: That's all right.

2. Call someone and get the wrong number. Use your imagination and the expressions below. Continue the conversation.

I think you have the wrong number.
There's no one here by that name.
You must have dialed the wrong number.

I'm sorry.
Sorry. Wrong number.
Oh, is this 555-1234?

A: Hello.
B: Hello. This is ______________.
Can I speak to ______________?
A: ________________________________
B: ________________________________

3. Practice.

Conversations

4. Focus on grammar. Review.

I'm They're He's	going to not going to	call the dentist. be in today. see a doctor.

5. What can you say?

They had an accident./ a tow truck

He has a toothache./ the dentist

She has a stomachache./ the doctor

There's a fire./ the fire department

6. Talk about emergencies. Use the words in 5.

A: What's the problem?

B: They had an accident.

A: What are they going to do?

B: They're going to call a tow truck.

Conversations

7. Practice.

Mary: Hello. Is Reuben there, please?
This is Mary Stern, his supervisor at work.
Steve: No, I'm sorry, he isn't.
Can I give him a message?
Mary: When is he going to be back?
Steve: I don't know. He's at the dentist.
Mary: I see. Please ask him to call me.

8. Focus on grammar.

Steve gave a message to	me.
	you.
	him.
	her.
	us.
	them.

Steve gave	me	a message.
	you	
	him	
	her	
	us	
	them	

9. Talk about the people.

A: What did she do?

B: She gave them a message.

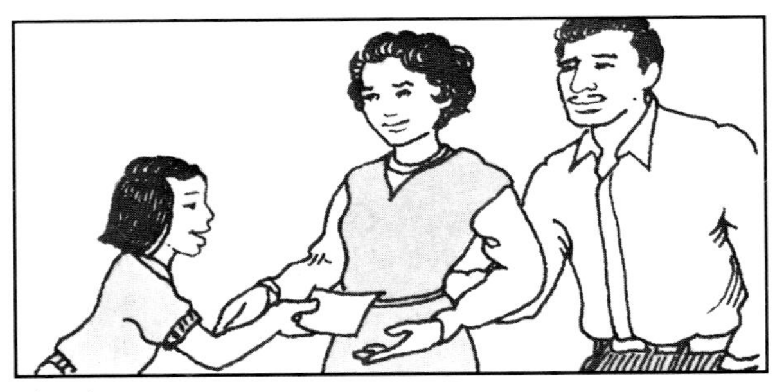

give/a message

give/the phone number

give/the phone book

give/change for the phone

Paperwork

1. Read the White and Yellow Pages from the phone books.

BRIDGETON WHITE PAGES	75	RESIDENCE	LINDSEY-LOPEZ
LINDSEY L 2938 Washington	**422-5678**	**LOPEZ Anna** 5239 Main	**433-1208**
LINDSEY R J 500 Ontario	**457-3396**	**LOPEZ B** 222 3rd	**406-1198**
LINDSEY T 3215 California	**490-2277**	**LOPEZ Beatrice** 58092 5th	**433-0821**
		LOPEZ M 5329 Main	**433-1208**

BRIDGETON DIRECT YELLOW PAGES	245 DENTISTS
WADE WAYNE 1532 Union	**559-2676**
WALKER EDNA ofc 303 Broadway	**436-1900**
res 25 2nd Ave	**484-6833**
WILSON KEVIN S 672 Grant St	**499-2774**
WONKA WILLIE W 3580 W. Main	**432-3838**
WOOD RUSSEL R 155 Cactus Circle	**419-6850**
WOODSIL ARNOLD P 606 Broadway	**436-2575**

b

2. Write the phone numbers for these people. Use the information in 1.

a. Kevin Wilson 499-2774
b. R. J. Lindsey ______
c. Edna Walker's office ______
d. Mario Lopez ______
e. Lois Lindsey ______
f. Thomas Lindsey ______

3. Add questions with your classmates. Then interview three classmates.

How often do you use the phone book? about two times a week

How often do you call directory assistance? once every two months

Why? when I want to get a number for someone in another area

How often do you make long-distance calls? once a month

To what places? Mexico

4. Pool your information. Then write summary sentences. (For example, *Eight students call directory assistance once a month.*)

Reading and Writing

1. What can you say about Tony?

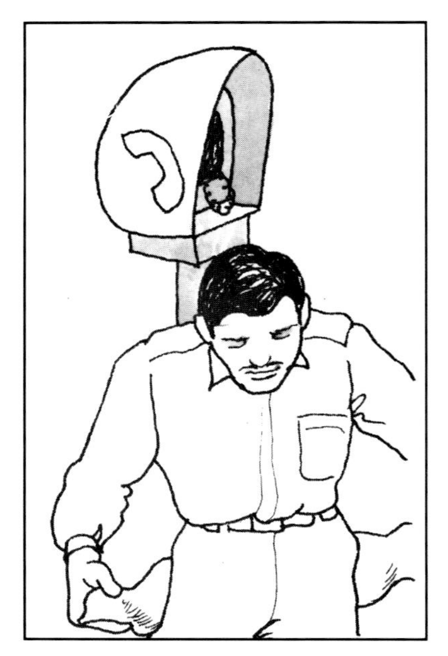

2. Read Tony's story. Circle a word you want to learn. Work with your classmates. Find out what it means.

Tony missed the bus today. It was his fault because he woke up late. He needed to find a public telephone. He had to call his boss.

First he ran to the phone booth on the corner. There was an "Out of Order" sign on the telephone.

Then he ran four blocks to another phone. He lifted the receiver, listened for the dial tone, and reached into his pocket for change. But he didn't have any change! It was in his jacket at home.

Tony ran to a drugstore and got change. At 9:15, he called work. He had to leave a message for his boss. Tony finally got to work at 9:45. He was very late.

3. Work in pairs.

Write two problems that were Tony's fault.

____

Write one problem that wasn't Tony's fault.

____

Why did Tony call his boss?

____

Interactions

Student A

1. Give information. You are a directory assistance operator.

A: Directory Assistance. What city, please?

B: Bridgeton. May I have the number for Larry Williams at 101 S. Broadway?

A: Hold on, please. That's 795-5071.

Johnson James J 535 Union . . . Bridgeton	**674-3669**
Johnson P L 1239 Washington Ct . . . Oldtown	**988-4443**
Jones Peter X 530 S Main . . . California City	**978-1990**
Robertson Mary Anna 66 W 3 Ave . . . Sea City	**980-8311**
Robertson Stanley H 2142 S Union . . . Bridgeton	**440-3136**
Rodriguez Francisco 782 S Union . . . Bridgeton	**331-3113**
Rodriguez Santiago 336 S Main . . . California City	**663-1440**
Tanaga Sumi 43 W 5 Ave . . . Sea City	**861-5071**
Tanaka Mike 3771 Elm . . . Mountain View	**399-5215**
Washington W 63950 W 8 Ave . . . Sea City	**861-6616**
Williams Andy & Beth 2767 Curtis Cir . . . Newtown	**644-1382**
Williams Larry P 101 S Broadway . . . Bridgeton	**795-5071**

e

2. Get information. B is a directory assistance operator. Ask for the phone numbers of these people. Write their numbers.

3. Find out how people answer the phone in your partner's country.

Interactions

Student B

e

1. Get information. A is a directory assistance operator. Ask for the phone numbers of these people. Write their numbers.

A: Directory Assistance. What city, please?

B: Bridgeton . May I have the number for Larry Williams at 101 S. Broadway?

A: Hold on, please. That's 795-5071 .

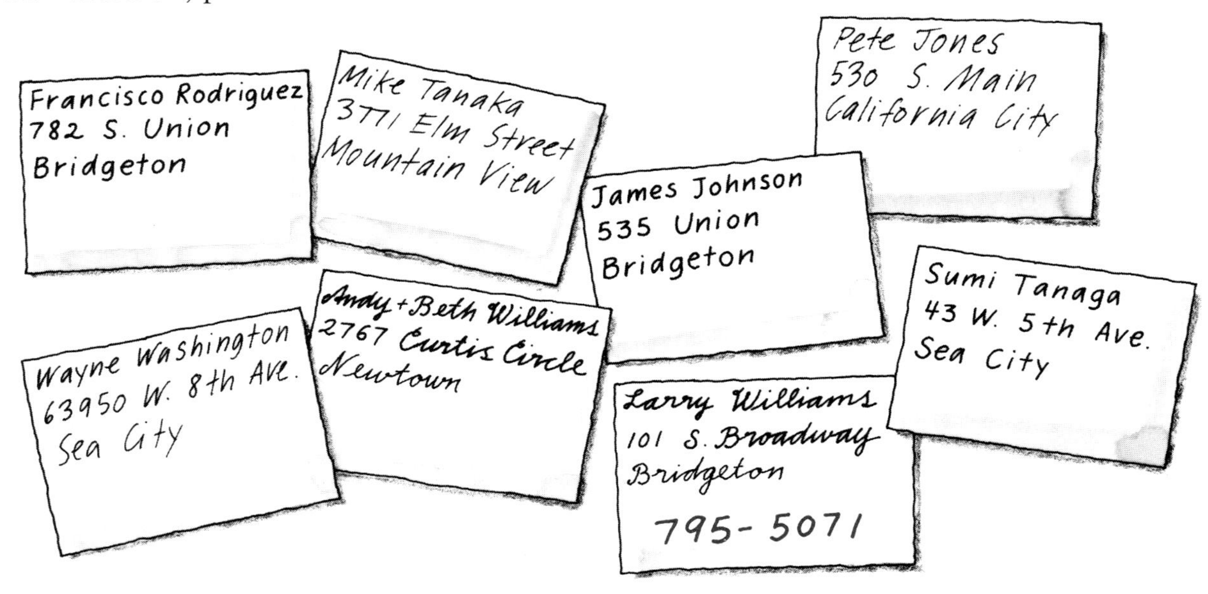

2. Give information. You are a directory assistance operator.

Chang Lee X 9468 Union . . . Bridgeton **794-3113**
Chang My Nhia 9470 Union . . . Bridgeton **794-8629**
Davis Alma V 7999 Main St . . . California City **978-6050**
Davis August R 8560 Union . . . Bridgeton **794-3233**
Evans Tim & Betty 104 Jefferson Pl . . . Bridgeton **709-1516**
Evans Manuel F off 300 S Main . . . California City **978-9778**
res 3206 S Washington . . . Bridgeton **605-2783**
Gomez Andres 3607 Elm . . . Mountain View **399-0147**
Gomez Roberta 3609 Elm . . . Mountain View **399-1626**
Harris Archie & Bev 5 Bridgeton Rd . . . Bridgeton **469-4237**
Harris Coleman Jr. 8135 Grant . . . Bridgeton **751-1687**
Harrison Zena Q 666 6th Ave . . . Sea City. **886-6666**
Harvey Mandy K 313 S 23 St . . . Brownsville **501-1667**

3. Find out how people answer the phone in your partner's country.

Progress Checks

1. **a** ☐ Respond appropriately when making or receiving a wrong-number call.

What are the people saying?

Do it yourself.

2. **c** ☐ Leave a short telephone message.
   d ☐ Take a short telephone message.

A, use your imagination. Leave a message with B. B, take a message.

3. **b** ☐ Use the phone book to find telephone numbers.

Look at the page in the phone book.

Dillon Laura	332 E 21	**987-9932**
Doe John	121 Washington	**764-2212**
Duggin J	443 Rio Rd. Sea City	**788-9019**
Dunn Jonathan	32 W 5	**798-9102**
Durran Frank	5528 S. Main	**572-8398**
Durran Martha	1776 Mt. Vernon	**223-4567**

Write the telephone numbers.

a. Martha Durran ______________ b. Clark Dooley ______________

c. Jonathan Dunn ______________ d. John Doe ______________

Progress Checks

4. **e** ☐ Call directory assistance to get a phone number.

What is the person saying?

Do it yourself.

Problem Solving

What's Joan's problem?

What should Joan do?
Now role play.

UNIT 4 The Supermarket

Getting Started

1. **Guess. Where are Devi and Ilona? What are they doing? What are they saying?**

2. **What can you hear?**

Conversations

1. Practice.

Devi: What do you need, Ilona?
Ilona: First, I have to return a carton of milk. Then I need some chicken, some frozen vegetables, and a few cleaning products. What about you?
Devi: I need some things from the deli, some detergent, and some paper towels. Oh, and a chocolate cake.
Ilona: I have an extra coupon for Marvel paper towels. Do you want it?
Devi: Thanks. See you in about 20 minutes.

2. What can you say?

Cleaning Products 2A

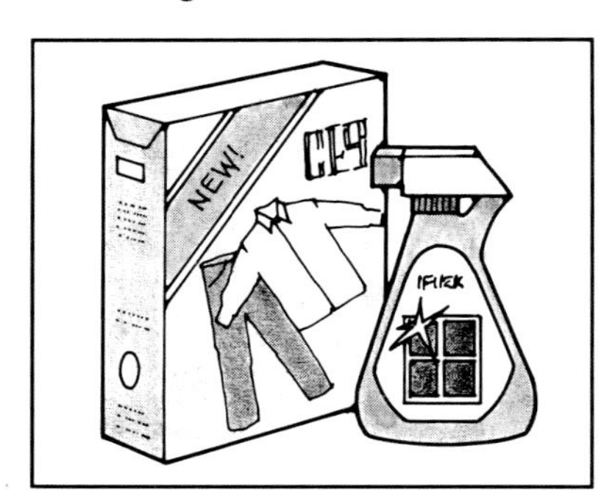

detergent/window cleaner

Frozen Foods 1A

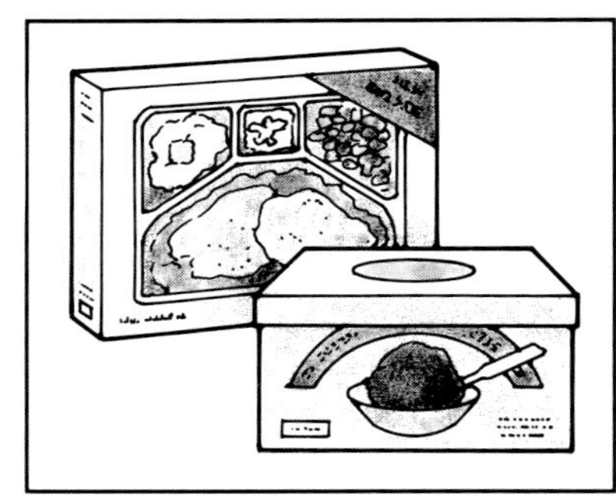

frozen dinner/ice cream

Paper Products 2B

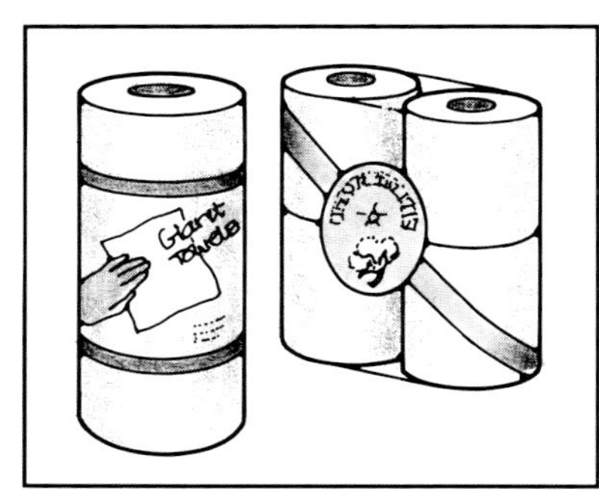

paper towels/ bathroom tissue

Canned Goods 5B

tuna/canned vegetables

Beverages 4B

soft drinks/juice

Snacks 5A

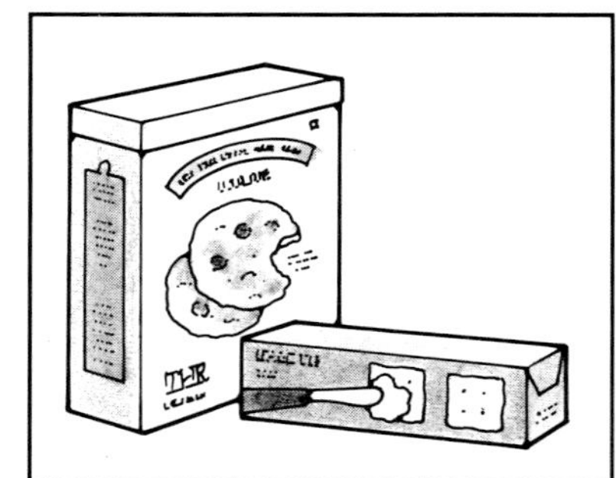

cookies/crackers

3. Ask for help in the supermarket. Use the items in 2.

A: Excuse me. Where can I find __detergent__?

B: In the __cleaning products__ section.

A: What aisle is that?

B: That's Aisle __2A__.

Conversations

4. Practice.

Ilona: Excuse me. I have a problem. I bought this milk yesterday. I poured a glass of milk last night and the milk was bad.
Clerk: I'm sorry. Let me see the expiration date. Hmm, December 2. That was two days ago.
Ilona: Here's my receipt.
Clerk: Do you want to get another carton?
Ilona: Yes, thanks.

5. Focus on grammar.

some	milk bread chicken

a	carton of milk loaf of bread package of chicken

a	glass of milk slice of bread piece of chicken

6. What can you say?

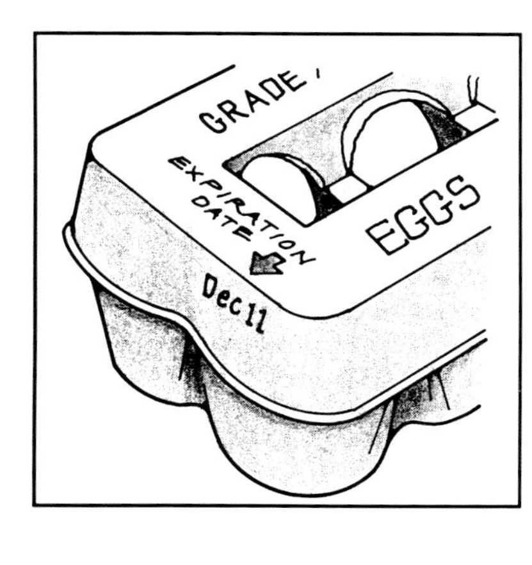

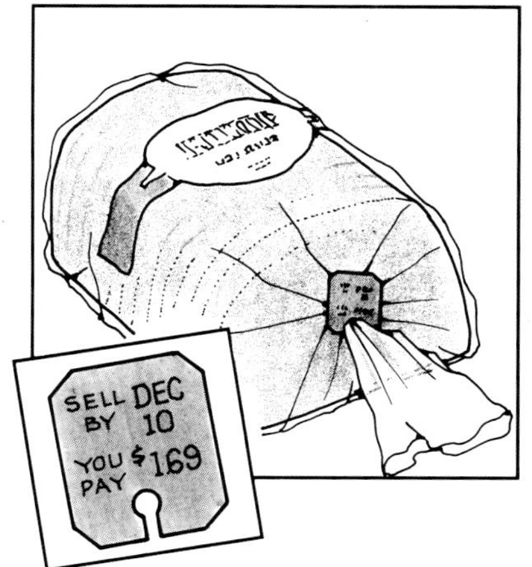

7. Return some bad food to the supermarket. Use the items in 6.

A: Excuse me. I have a problem. I bought <u>these eggs</u> yesterday and <u>they're</u> bad. Here's my receipt.

B: I'm sorry. Let me see the expiration date. Hmm, <u>December 11</u>. That was two days ago. Do you want to get another <u>carton</u>?

A: Yes, thanks. OR No, I'd like a refund, please.

Conversations

8. Practice.

Devi:	Pardon me. Can you hand me that box of detergent, please?
Clerk:	Do you want the big box? It's a better buy.
Devi:	Really?
Clerk:	Yes. Here, look at the unit prices. The small box is more expensive. It costs almost 50¢ a pound. The big box costs about 43¢ a pound.
Devi:	I see. Thanks.

9. Focus on grammar.

big	bigger than
cheap	cheaper than

bad	worse than
good	better than

expensive	more expensive than
convenient	more convenient than

10. Talk about the supermarket items. Use these words.

nutritious   sweet   convenient   cheap   delicious

A: Which do you like better, apples or oranges?

B: Apples. They're more delicious than oranges.

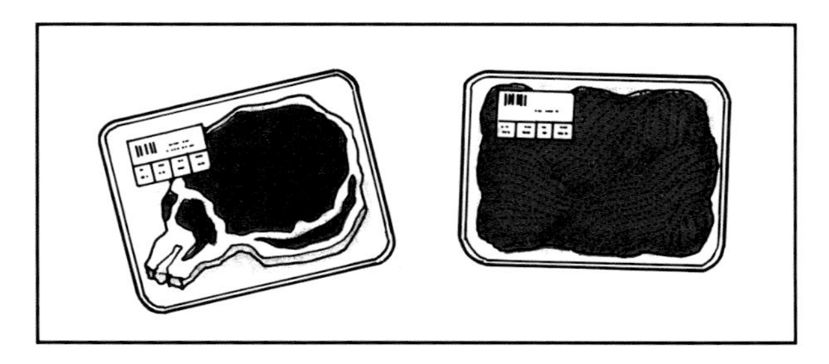

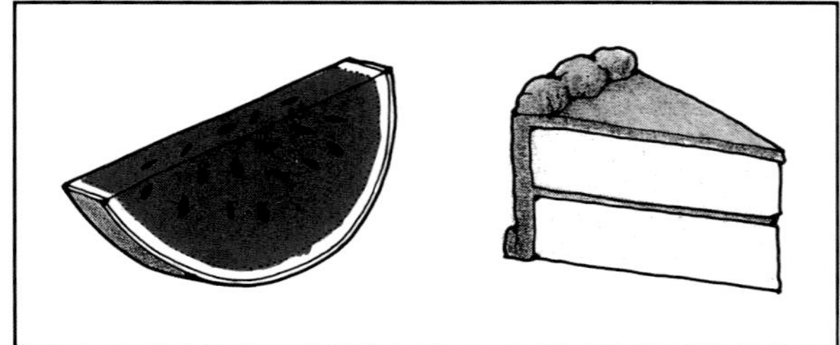

Paperwork

1. Read the unit pricing labels.

C

2. Write the answers.

	Total Cost	*Cost of 1 Qt.*
a. Eve's 64-ounce apple juice	$1.89	________
Sunny 64-ounce apple juice	________	________
Eve's 32-ounce apple juice	________	________
Sunny 48-ounce apple juice	________	________

b. Which brand costs less per quart, the Eve's 64-ounce bottle or the Sunny 64-ounce bottle? ________________

c. Which brand costs more per quart, the Sunny 48-ounce bottle or the Sunny 64-ounce bottle? ________________

3. Add questions with your classmates. Then interview three classmates.

Where does your family shop for food? at Lucky Seven

Why do they shop there? It's near my house and it's cheap.

Who does the food shopping in your family? my children and I

________________?

4. Pool your information. Then write summary sentences.

Reading and Writing

d

1. Work in pairs. Label the sections. Use these words:

Bakery   Dairy   Deli   Fish   Meat   Poultry   Produce

2. Work in pairs. What foods are in each section? Write three foods you know.

Bakery	bread	______	______
Dairy	______	______	______
Deli	______	______	______
Fish	______	______	______
Meat	______	______	______
Poultry	______	______	______
Produce	______	______	______

Reading and Writing

3. **What can you say about these shopping habits?**

4. **Read about being a smart shopper. Circle a word you want to learn. Work with your classmates. Find out what it means.**

How to Be a Smart Shopper

Are you a smart shopper? See how many of these things you do.

• **Clip coupons**. Smart shoppers clip coupons from newspapers and ads. They take the coupons to the store and look for the products in the coupons. They can usually save a few dollars a week.

• **Read unit pricing labels.** Smart shoppers look at the unit price for each item. Sometimes products come in two sizes. Smart shoppers check the unit prices and usually buy the size with the lower unit price. Sometimes there are two brands. Smart shoppers check the unit prices and usually buy the cheaper brand.

• **Read expiration dates.** Smart shoppers look at the expiration dates on packages of meat, fish, poultry, dairy products, and baked goods. Sometimes two quarts of milk have different dates stamped on them. Smart shoppers always buy the fresher milk.

5. **Work with your group. What are some other good shopping habits and other ways to save money?**

6. **Pick one of your ideas in 5 and write a paragraph about it. Use the paragraphs in 4 as examples.**

7. **Read your paragraph to your group.**

8. **What has surprised you about shopping for food in the U.S.? Write about it.**

Listening Plus

1. **Notice the difference.**
   Point.
   Listen and write the sentences.

You see...	*but you hear...*
...cup of...	*...cuhpuh...*
...bowl of...	*...bowluh...*

a. ______________________

b. ______________________

2. **Point.**
   Number.

THE BEST IN THE WEST AISLE DIRECTORY

ITEM	AISLE	ITEM	AISLE
Beverages	___	Potato Chips	15B
Brooms	1B	Soup, Canned & Dry	10A
Cookies	5A	Tissue, Bathroom	2B
Crackers	___	Toothpaste	3A
Detergent, Laundry	2B	Towels, Paper	2B
Dinners, Frozen	6A	Tuna, Canned	11B
Ice Cream	6B	Vegetables, Canned	___

3. **Fill in the information.**

	Produce	*Meat*	*Bakery*	*Deli*	*Dairy*
Nancy			cake		
Jeff					
Tim					

4. **What about you?**

____

Interactions

Student A

1. **Get information. Ask B the prices of items at Foodsmart.**

   A: How much is Foodsmart Cola?

   B: It's 99¢ for a 2-liter bottle.

   A: 99¢? Thanks.

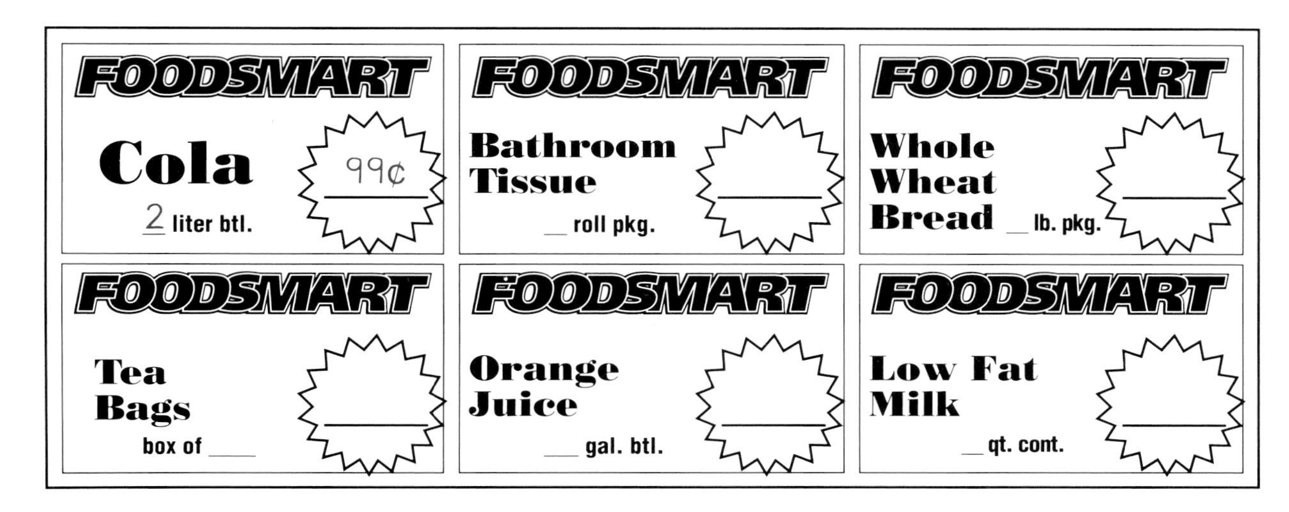

2. **Give information. Tell B the prices of the items at Best in the West Markets.**

f

3. **Work with your partner. Compare prices. Which supermarket is more expensive?** ______________________

4. **Find out about the prices of food in your partner's country.**

Interactions

Student B

1. **Give information. Tell A the prices of items at Foodsmart.**

   A: How much is Foodsmart Cola?

   B: It's 99¢ for a 2-liter bottle.

   A: 99¢? Thanks.

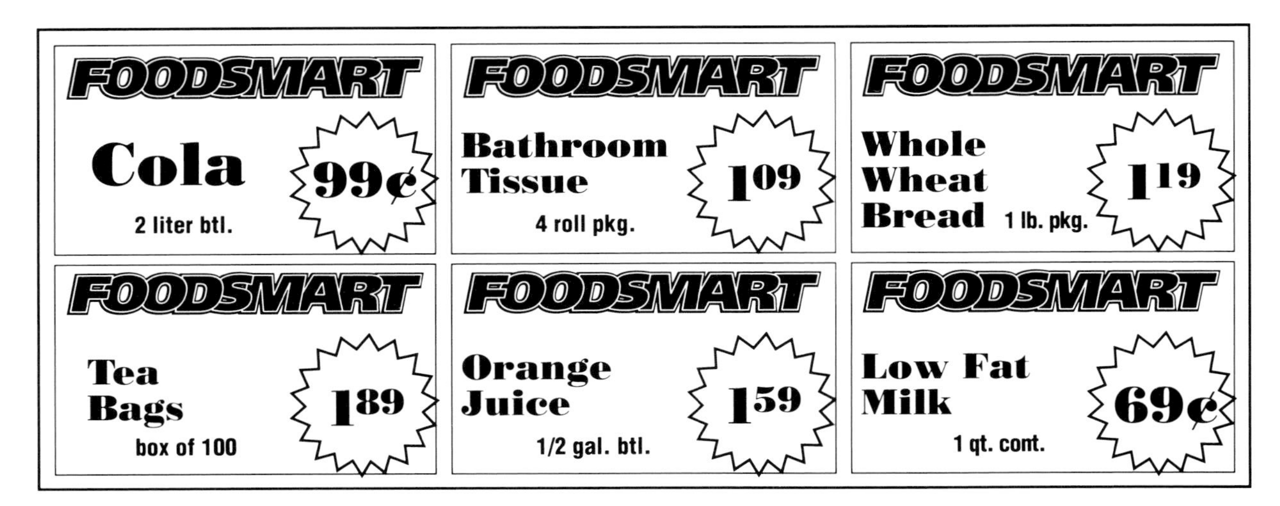

2. **Get information. Ask A the prices of the items at Best in the West Markets.**

f

3. **Work with your partner. Compare prices. Which supermarket is more expensive?** ____________________

4. **Find out about the prices of food in your partner's country.**

Progress Checks

1. d ☐ Read signs for store sections in a supermarket to locate items.
e ☐ Read aisle directories in a supermarket to locate items.

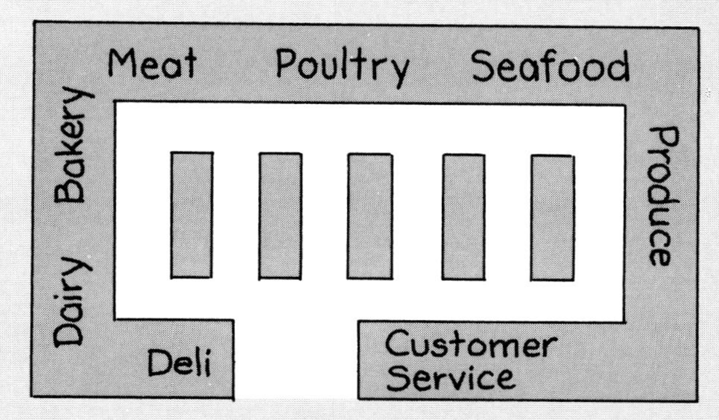

BEST IN THE WEST AISLE DIRECTORY

ITEM	AISLE
Beverages	16A
Brooms	1B
Cookies	5A
Crackers	14B
Detergent, Laundry	2B
Dinners, Frozen	6A
Ice Cream	6B

Look at the store sections.
Write the section for the items.

Milk ________________ section

Lettuce ________________ section

Cake ________________ section

Look at the aisle directory.
Write aisle numbers for the items.

Orange juice Aisle ____

Mops and Brooms Aisle ____

Butter cookies Aisle ____

2. a ☐ Read expiration dates on food items.

Circle the items that are fresher.

CHICKEN DRUMSTICKS

OCT. 15

NET WEIGHT	PRICE PER LB	TOTAL PRICE
1.35 lbs	$1.29	$1.75

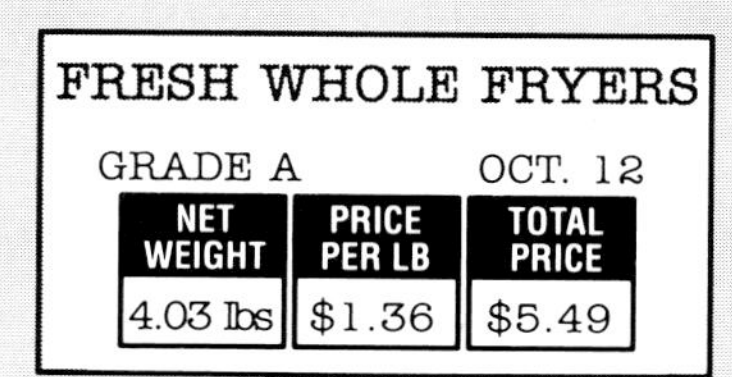

3. b ☐ Express a need to return or exchange an item.

What are the people saying?

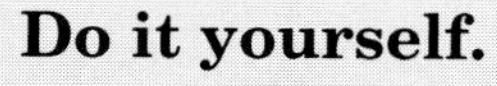

Do it yourself.

Progress Checks

4. **c** ☐ Read unit pricing labels in a supermarket for comparison shopping.
f ☐ Read supermarket ads for comparison shopping.

WHITE WAVE LAUNDRY DETERGENT

42 oz. **.09 per oz.** **$3.78**

a. Which box of White Wave Laundry Detergent costs less per pound?__________

b. Which is cheaper per pound, Foodsmart Detergent or White Wave?__________

Problem Solving

What's Julie's problem?

What should Julie do?
Now role play.

UNIT

5 Health

Getting Started

1. Guess. Where are Arturo and Miss Chen? What are they doing? What are they saying?

2. What can you hear?

Conversations

1. Practice.

Miss Chen:	Doctor's office.
Arturo:	Hello. This is Arturo Mendoza. I'd like to make an appointment.
Miss Chen:	Why do you need to see the doctor?
Arturo:	I have a pain in my stomach.
Miss Chen:	Are you in pain now?
Arturo:	Yes. But it's not too bad.
Miss Chen:	When did the pain start?
Arturo:	About a week ago.
Miss Chen:	I see. Can you come in at 5:30 tomorrow?
Arturo:	Sure. Tomorrow is fine. Thank you.

2. What can you say?

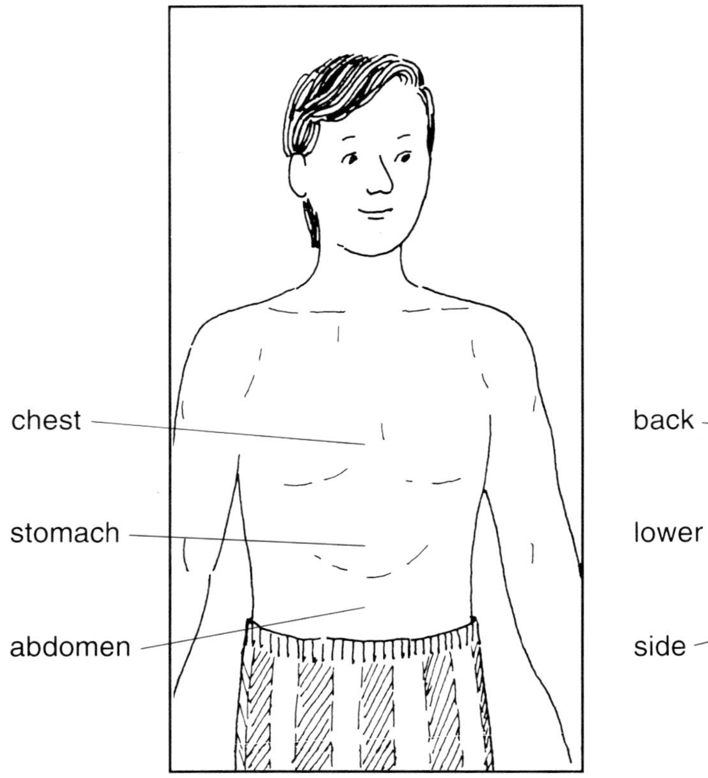

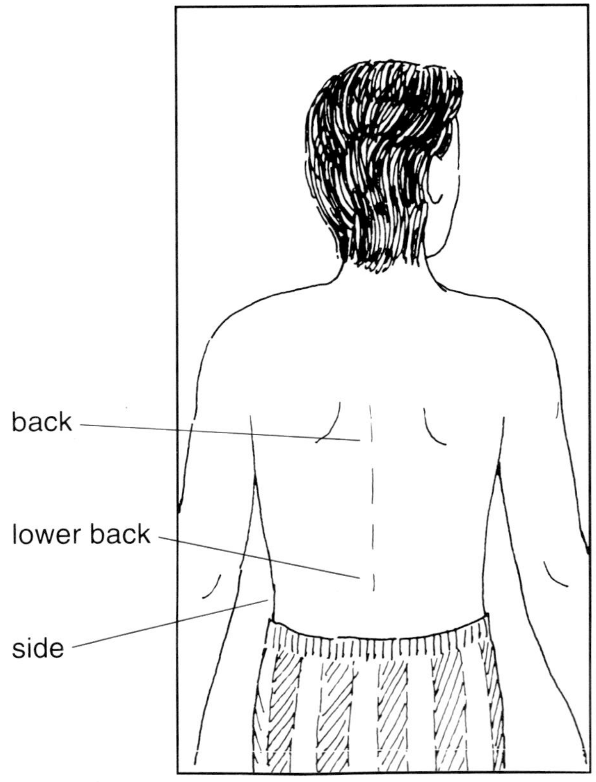

3. Make a doctor's appointment. Use the conversation in 1 and the words in 2.

A: Doctor's office.

B: Hello. This is ________________. I'd like to make an appointment.

A: ______________________________________.

Conversations

4. Practice.

Miss Chen: Doctor's office.
Arturo: This is Arturo Mendoza. I called this morning. I have to change my appointment.
Miss Chen: OK. When was your appointment?
Arturo: Tomorrow at 5:30.
Miss Chen: And when do you want to come in?
Arturo: How about the day after tomorrow?
Miss Chen: OK. That's Thursday. How's 2:00?
Arturo: Does the doctor have evening hours on Thursday?
Miss Chen: Yes, he does. How's 7:00?
Arturo: That's fine. Thank you.

5. What can you say?

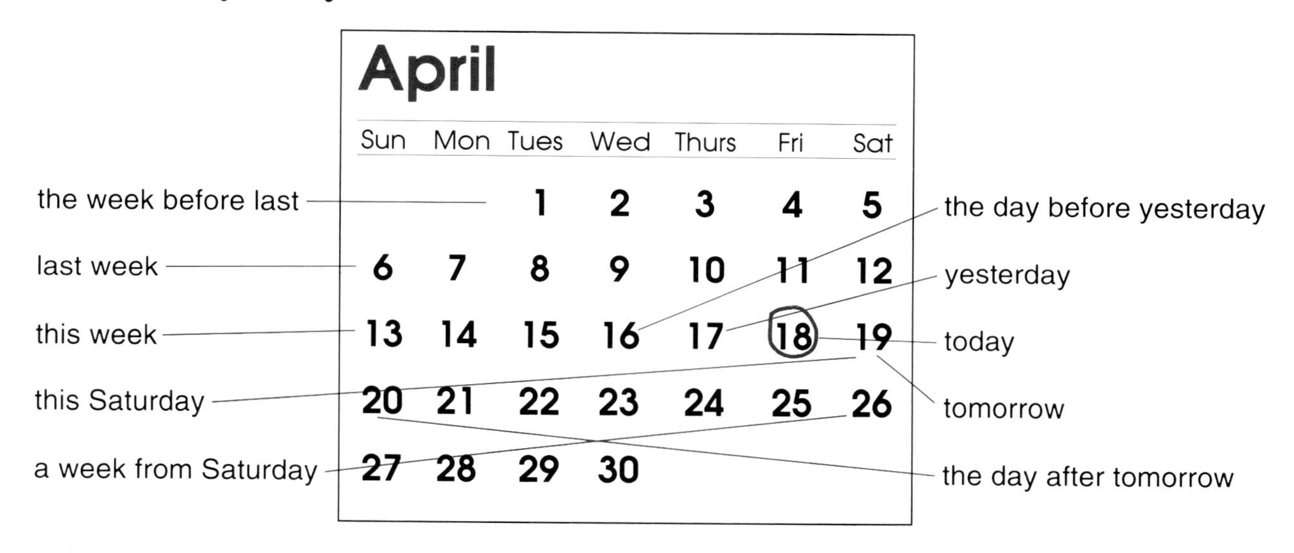

b **6. Change a doctor's appointment. Use the words in 5.**

A: Doctor's office.

B: Yes. This is ____________. I called last week.

I have to change my appointment.

A: OK. When was your appointment?

B: This Wednesday at 3:30.

A: And when do you want to come in?

B: How about a week from Monday?

A: ____________.

Conversations

7. Practice.

Arturo:	Here's the form.
Miss Chen:	Thank you. Oh, Mr. Mendoza, you forgot to fill in the information about surgery.
Arturo:	Sorry. Um, in July I fell and hurt my knee, and I had an operation.
Miss Chen:	Uh-huh. And do you have any allergies?
Arturo:	Yes. I'm allergic to penicillin.
Miss Chen:	Any other allergies?
Arturo:	I got a rash from strawberries once, but it went away quickly.

8. Focus on grammar.

forget	fall	hurt	have	get	go
forgot	fell	hurt	had	got	went

9. Talk about the people.

A: What happened?

B: He hurt his leg ________.

hurt

go

get

have

Paperwork

1. **What can you say about the medical history form?**

+ MEDICAL HISTORY FORM +

Name ______________________ Birth Date __/__/__

Address ______________________ Phone (____) ______

______________________ Sex ____ M ____ F

Do you have Medicaid? ____ Yes ____ No Other insurance? ____ Yes ____ No

Health Insurance Carrier ______________________

Medicaid or Policy Number ______________________

Previous or current health problems: (Please check ✓)

____ Appendicitis	____ Frequent Colds	____ Kidney Trouble
____ Cancer	____ Heart Disease	____ Tuberculosis
____ Diabetes	____ High Blood Pressure	____ Ulcers

Surgery, if any

______________________ Date ________

______________________ Date ________

Do you have any allergies? Please specify.

____

c 2. **Fill in the form.**

d 3. **Add questions with your classmates. Then interview three classmates.**

Do you have Medicaid or other health insurance?

I have Liberty Mutual health insurance.

Did you have health insurance in your home country?

no

Do you have any allergies? I'm allergic to aspirin.

______________________?

4. **Pool your information. Then write summary sentences.**

Reading and Writing

1. **What can you say about the chart?**

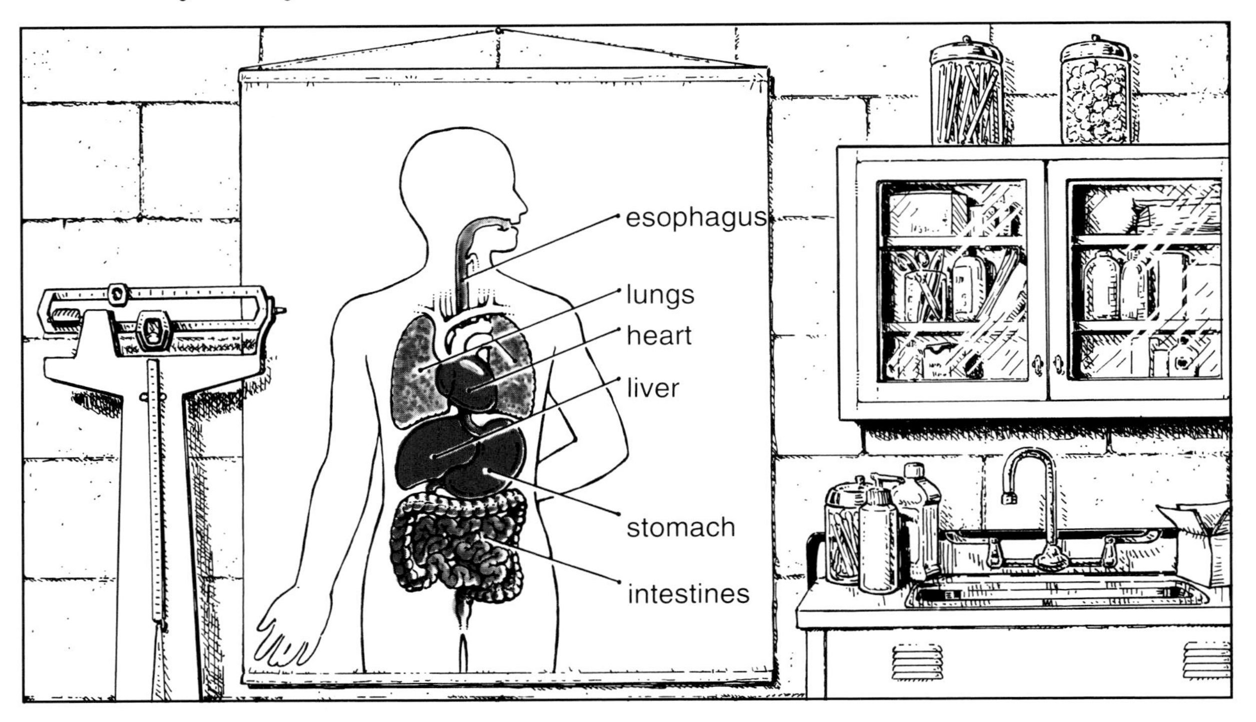

2. **Read Arturo's story. Circle a word you want to learn. Work with your classmates. Find out what it means.**

Arturo had an appointment with Dr. Woo yesterday. The doctor examined him. First he listened to his heart and lungs. They were fine. Then he took his temperature and blood pressure. His temperature was normal, but his blood pressure was a little high. After that, Dr. Woo examined Arturo's stomach, and Arturo felt some pain.

Arturo was nervous. "Am I going to need an operation?" he asked.

"I don't know yet. I don't see any big problems," said Dr. Woo, "but I want to do some tests. After the tests, I can tell you more."

"OK, Dr. Woo," said Arturo.

3. **Work in pairs. Complete these sentences.**

a. Arturo's heart and lungs were ______________________________.

b. His temperature was ______________, but his blood pressure was

______________________________.

c. He had a pain in his ______________________________.

d. He felt ____________________ about his problem.

Reading and Writing

4. What can you say about the greeting cards?

a. Get Well Card

b. Baby Congratulations Card

c. Sympathy Card

5. Work in pairs. Match the sentences or phrases to the greeting cards in 4. Write the letters of the greeting cards in the blanks.

__b__ Congratulations on the birth of your baby.

____ Best wishes for a rapid recovery.

____ We miss you! Get well soon.

____ Our prayers are with you in this time of sadness.

____ I was so sorry to hear of your loss.

____ How wonderful to have a new little son!

6. Work in small groups. On a separate piece of paper, write other greeting card sentences and phrases you know.

7. Write a note or make a greeting card to send to a friend in the hospital.

8. Read your note or card to your group.

9. What has surprised you about going to the doctor in the U.S.? Write about it.

Listening Plus

1. Notice the difference.
Point.
Listen and write the sentences.

You see...	***but you hear...***
...have to...	*...haftuh...*
...has to...	*...hastuh...*

a. ______________________________

b. ______________________________

2. Point.
Check.

✓ Appendicitis
___ Cancer
___ Diabetes
___ Frequent Colds
___ Heart Disease
___ High Blood Pressure
___ Kidney Trouble
___ Tuberculosis
___ Ulcers

Surgery, if any: ______________________________

3. Fill in the information.

	Health Problem	***Day***	***Date***	***Time***
Richard	backache			
Margaret				
Tyrone				

4. What about you?

____

Interactions
Student A

1. **Get information. Student B is a doctor's receptionist. First, call the doctor's office to make an appointment. Then, call again to change it. Listen to B. Choose the appropriate response. Today is Monday, March 5.**

   1. Hello. This is ______________________. I'd like to make an appointment.
      OR
      This is ______________________. I called earlier today. I have to change my appointment.

   2. The day after tomorrow at 10:00.
      OR
      I have a pain in my lower back.

   3. Yes. But it's not too bad.
      OR
      How about a week from today?

   4. Hmm. Does the doctor have morning hours?
      OR
      About two days ago.

   5. That's fine. Thank you.
      OR
      The day after tomorrow? Yes, I can.

   Circle the date on the calendar for the first appointment. Check your answer with your partner.

March

Sun	Mon	Tues	Wed	Thurs	Fri	Sat
				1	2	3
4	5	6	7	8	9	10
11	12	13	14	15	16	17
18	19	20	21	22	23	24
25	26	27	28	29	30	31

2. **Find out about doctors in your partner's country.**

Interactions

Student B

1. Give information. You are the doctor's receptionist. Student A is calling to make an appointment. Listen to A and choose the appropriate response.
Today is Monday, March 5.

1. OK. When was your appointment?
   OR
   Why do you need to see the doctor?

2. Are you in pain now?
   OR
   And when do you want to come in?

3. OK. How's 5:00?
   OR
   When did the pain start?

4. Yes. How's 10:00?
   OR
   Can you come in at 10:00 the day after tomorrow?

5. OK. See you in a week.
   OR
   OK. See you the day after tomorrow.

Fill in the appointment card for the second appointment. Check your answer with your partner.

M ______________________________
has an appointment with
Mark Silver, M.D.
Day Wednesday Date 3/7
At 10 (a.m.)/p.m.
Please notify office 24 hours before if you cannot keep this appointment.

2. Find out about doctors in your partner's country.

Progress Checks

1. **c** ☐ Fill in a medical history form.
d ☐ Respond to questions about health insurance.

Fill in this form.

Name: ______________________________ Date of Birth: ___/___/___
Last First

Do you have Medicaid? ____ Yes ____ No Other insurance? ____ Yes ____ No

Health Insurance Carrier: ______________________________

Medicaid or Policy Number: ______________________________

Previous or current health problems: (Please check ✓)

____ Appendicitis	____ Frequent Colds	____ Kidney Trouble
____ Cancer	____ Heart Disease	____ Tuberculosis
____ Diabetes	____ High Blood Pressure	____ Ulcers

Have you ever had surgery? Give reasons and dates. ______________________________

____

Do you have any allergies? ______________________________

2. **a** ☐ Make a doctor's appointment on the telephone.

What are the people saying?

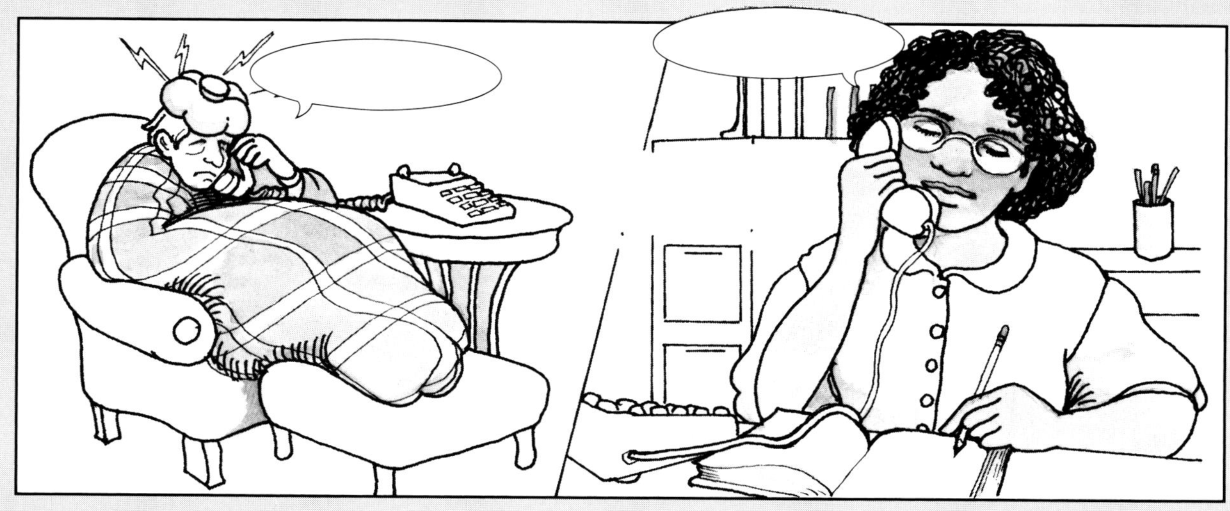

Do it yourself.

Progress Checks

3. b ☐ Change or cancel a doctor's appointment.

What are the people saying?

Do it yourself.

Problem Solving

What's Betty's problem?

What should Betty do?
Now role play.

UNIT

6 Housing

Getting Started

1. **Guess. Where are Reuben, his roommates, and Mr. Banks? What are they doing? What are they saying?**

2. **What can you hear?**

Conversations

1. Practice.

Reuben: OK. We'll take the apartment.
Mr. Banks: All three of you?
Reuben: Yes. Is that OK?
Mr. Banks: Well, yes, but no more than three.
Reuben: No problem, Mr. Banks. When will the apartment be available?
Mr. Banks: The first of the month. When can you bring in the security deposit?
Reuben: Hmm. I won't have time tomorrow. How about the day after tomorrow? I'll get a certified check and bring it with the lease.
Mr. Banks: Fine.

2. What can you say?

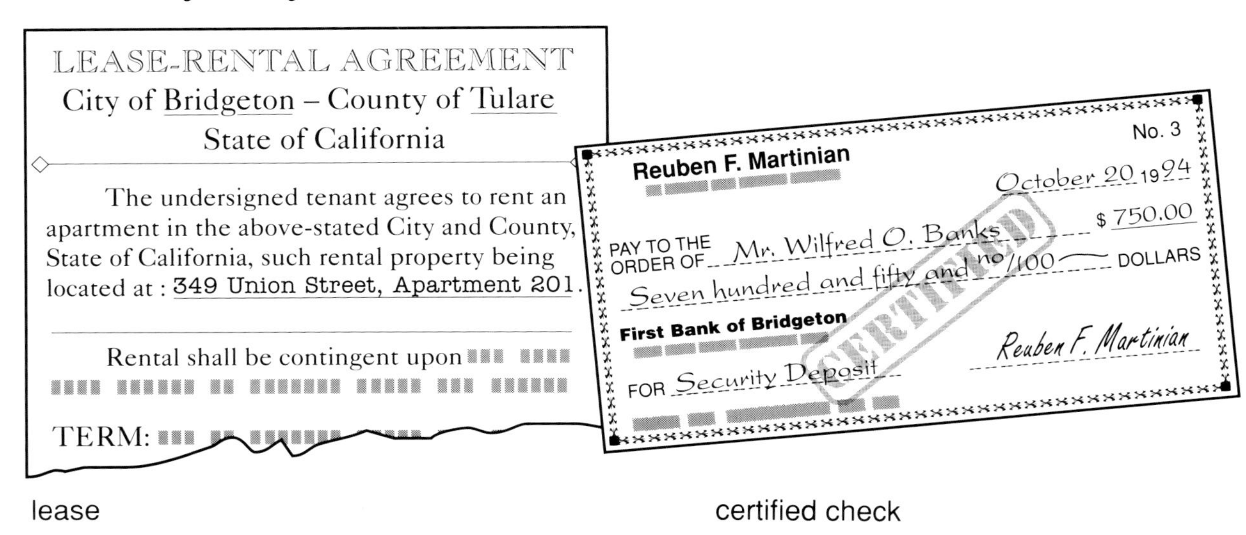

lease

certified check

3. Focus on grammar.

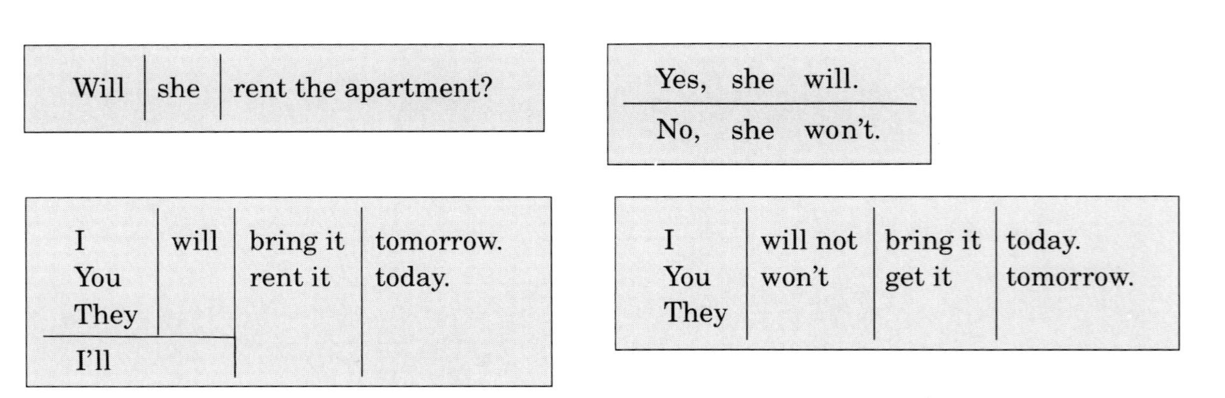

Will	she	rent the apartment?

Yes,	she	will.
No,	she	won't.

I You They	will	bring it rent it	tomorrow. today.
I'll			

I You They	will not won't	bring it get it	today. tomorrow.

4. Rent an apartment. Use the conversation in 1.

Conversations

5. Practice.

Reuben: By the way, what's the nearest supermarket?
Mr. Banks: Grand Foods. It's on Lincoln and 12th.
Reuben: That's good. And is there a hardware store near here? We need some tools.
Mr. Banks: The closest hardware store is on Park and 28th. They have the best prices.
Reuben: Oh, yeah, I know the place. Ron's. It's the biggest hardware store in Bridgeton.
Mr. Banks: Uh-huh. It's also the busiest hardware store in Bridgeton.
Reuben: Well, thanks Mr. Banks. See you tomorrow.

6. Focus on grammar.

near	the nearest
busy	the busiest
good	the best

big

the biggest

7. Talk about your community.

A: Where is the nearest bus stop?
B: ______________.

a. near/bus stop b. big/pharmacy c. nice/park
b. good/bookstore e. busy/supermarket f. cheap/video store

Conversations

8. **Practice.**

Reuben:	What are the start-up costs for electricity, please?
Ms. Wahl:	We'll need a $50 deposit. And you'll have to pay an installation fee of $13.
Reuben:	OK.
Ms. Wahl:	What's your new address?
Reuben:	349 Union Street, Apartment 201.
Ms. Wahl:	When do you want electric service to start?
Reuben:	We're going to move in on the first.
Ms. Wahl:	Fine. We'll send a representative. Will you be there between 8:00 a.m. and 5:00 p.m. on November 1?
Reuben:	Yes. Someone will be there all day.
Ms. Wahl:	Very good. Thank you for calling Bridgeton Electric and Gas.

9. **What can you say?**

Utility	Deposit	Installation Fee
Electricity	$50	$13
Gas	$20	$ 5
Telephone	None	$42

C

10. **Get utilities installed. Use the conversation in 8 and the information in 9.**

Paperwork

1. Read the housing ads.

2 LG BR, unfurn, new kit, DR, nr trans, school. No pets. Util incl. $675, 1 mo dep. Downtown. Call (209) 703-2667

3 BR hse, 1 1/2 ba, kids, stv/frig, W/D, $1285 w/1 yr lease. Wind River area. Call (209) 681-7466

Bridgeton Heights, $750 1 BR + lg LR, new w/w cpt, a/c, elev, pkg, senior bldg. 2 mo. sec dep. (209) 910-9106

d

2. Write the abbreviations from 1 for these words.

Kinds of Housing and Rooms		***Things Housing Can Come With***		***Useful Words***	
apartment	apt.	air conditioning	____	included	____
bathroom	____	elevator	____	large	____
bedroom	____	furnished	____	month	____
building	____	parking	____	near	____
dining room	____	stove/refrigerator	____	security deposit	____
house	____	utilities	____	transportation	____
kitchen	____	wall-to-wall carpeting	____	unfurnished	____
living room	____	washer/dryer	____	with	____

3. Add questions with your classmates. Then interview three classmates.

What part of town do you live in? the Millbank section

What utilities are included in your rent? water

Look at the second column.

What did your house come with? stove and refrigerator

____________________?

4. Pool your information. Then write summary sentences.

Reading and Writing

1. **What can you say about Reuben's phone bill?**

BT
BRIDGETON TELEPHONE

BILL DATE: Nov. 25
ACCOUNT NUMBER: (209) 378-4242

REUBEN F. MARTINIAN
349 UNION ST., APT. 201
BRIDGETON, CA 93208

PREVIOUS BALANCE	$16.88
INSTALLATION FEE	42.00
CURRENT CHARGES	24.65
TOTAL AMOUNT DUE	$83.53

2. **Read Reuben's story. Circle a word you want to learn. Work with your classmates. Find out what it means.**

Today Reuben got the first bill for his new telephone service. He looked at the total amount due, and he was surprised. It was $83.53! Then he saw the previous balance of $16.88, and he called the phone company.

"Hello. This is Reuben Martinian. I have a problem with my telephone bill. My phone service started two weeks ago, but today I got a bill with a previous balance."

"Just a minute, please. What's your phone number? I'll look up your account," the phone company representative said.

"My phone number is 378-4242," Reuben replied.

"I'm sorry, Mr. Martinian. We made a mistake. I'll deduct $16.88 from your bill. With your installation fee of $42.00 and your current charges, the total amount due is $66.65. I apologize for the inconvenience."

"Thank you," Reuben said.

3. **Work in pairs. Answer these questions.**

a. Why was Reuben surprised?
b. What did Reuben do about his problem?
c. How much should the phone bill be?
d. Who made a mistake?

Progress Checks

1. d ☐ Read housing ads.

1	2	3
area. (209) 555-7389	area. (209) 555-7389	2 yr lease. Westside area. (209) 555-7389
2 BR, unfurn, new kit, a/c, nr trans, school. Util incl $725, 1 mo dep. 130 Union St. Call (209) 703-2667	2 BR hse, 1 ba, stv/frig, W/D, drapes, w/w cpt. $1234, w/2 yr lease. Westside area. (209) 681-7466	$1050 2 BR, w/w cpt. nr shopping, no pets, elev, pkg. Sec dep. (209) 910-9106
3 BR hse, stv/frig,	3 BR hse, stv/frig,	3 BR hse, stv/frig, W/D, drapes, w/w cpt.

Fill in the blanks. Write the number or numbers of the ads.

a. You need an apartment in a building with an elevator. ________________

b. You want an apartment near a school for your child. ________________

c. You want a house with wall-to-wall carpeting. ________________

2. a ☐ Ask about basic conditions for renting an apartment or house.
b ☐ Ask about accessibility to community services and transportation.

What are the people saying?

Do it yourself.

3. e ☐ Write a letter of complaint about a housing problem.

Choose a problem and write to a landlord or manager about it.

Progress Checks

4. **C** ☐ Arrange for installation of household utilities.

What are the people saying?

Do it yourself.

Problem Solving

What's Emma and Bill's problem?

What should Emma and Bill do?
Now role play.

UNIT 7

Finding a Job

Getting Started

1. Guess. Where are Binh and Mr. Hale? What are they doing? What are they saying?

2. What can you hear?

Conversations

1. Practice.

Mr. Hale: Mr. Vo, I'm Bob Hale.
Binh: How do you do?
Mr. Hale: Please have a seat.
Binh: Thank you.
Mr. Hale: Now, what job are you interested in?
Binh: I'm looking for a job as a carpenter.
Mr. Hale: A carpenter? That's interesting.
Binh: Yes. I like to work with wood, and I know how to use power tools.

2. Focus on grammar. Review of *can* and *like to*.

He	knows how likes	to	work with wood. use power tools.
	can		

3. What can you say? Add other words you know.

gardener/work with plants
use garden tools

office assistant/work with people
operate office machines

day care worker/work with people
take care of children

mechanic/work with cars
repair brakes

4. Ask about getting a job. Use the conversation in 1 and the words in 3.

Conversations

5. Practice.

Mr. Hale: Do you have any experience as a carpenter?
Binh: Yes. I was a carpenter in Vietnam for three years, from 1965 to 1968.
Mr. Hale: Where did you get your training?
Binh: I worked in my family's business. I learned on the job.
Mr. Hale: Do you use carpentry skills in your job now?
Binh: Well, right now I use my carpentry skills for repair work.
Mr. Hale: For example?
Binh: I replace broken windows and change locks.

6. What can you say?

cook/1985–1990
in vocational school

factory worker/1982–1986
on the job

tailor/1985–1989
in a refugee camp

teacher's aide/1990–1991
at a community college

data entry operator/1983–1988
in a technical school

repairperson/1989–1992
in high school

7. Talk about the people in 6.

A: Does he have any experience?

B: Yes. He was a cook for 5 years, from 1985 to 1990.

A: Where did he get his training?

A: In vocational school.

Conversations

8. Practice.

Mr. Hale: Why should a company hire you, Mr. Vo? What are your strengths?
Binh: Well, I'm a hard worker, and I learn quickly.
Mr. Hale: Anything else?
Binh: Yes. I'm honest and dependable, and I work neatly and carefully.
Mr. Hale: Very good. I'm going to send you on an interview at L.N. Construction Company. They need a carpenter's helper.
Binh: Thank you very much, Mr. Hale.
Mr. Hale: You bet.

9. Focus on grammar.

She is	careful.
	neat.
	quick.
	a good worker.
	a hard worker.
	never late.

She	works carefully.
	neatly.
	quickly.
	well with people.
	hard.
	never comes late.

10. Talk about the people.

A: Why should a company hire Jane?
B: She's neat, and she works carefully.

a. Jane neat/carefully

b. Otto never late/well with people

c. Lisbeth dependable/quickly

d. Paul hard worker/neatly

11. Talk about yourself. Use the conversation in 8.

Paperwork

1. **Read the job application form.**

APPLICATION FOR EMPLOYMENT

Name ______________________________ Soc. Sec. No. ______ – ______ – ______
Last First

Address ______________________________ Phone ( ) ______________

____

Are you legally able to work in the U.S.? Yes ___ No ___

Are you 18 years or older? Yes ___ No ___ Position desired ______________

Employment History (List last job first.)

Employer Name and Address	Dates	From / To	Position	Salary	Job Duties

Education and Training

School	Location	No. of Years	Subjects	Graduate?
Elementary				
High School				
College				
Other				

I declare that the above information is true and correct to the best of my knowledge.

Signature: ______________________________ Date: ______________

c 2. **Fill in the form.**

d 3. **Add questions with your classmates. Then interview three classmates.**

Are you working now? yes

What do you do? I'm a cook.

What schools did you attend in your country? elementary school and high school

What was the last school you attended? Westside Community Adult School

______________________________?

4. **Pool your information. Then write summary sentences.**

Reading and Writing

1. **What can you say about Elena's job skills?**

2. **Elena and Natalya are friends. Read Elena's story. Circle a word you want to learn. Work with your classmates. Find out what it means.**

"Natalya," Elena said, "I'm worried. I need a job."

"What kind of job do you want?" Natalya asked.

"What kind of job can I get? I don't have any job experience, and I don't have any job skills," she said.

"Oh, Elena, you're a homemaker. You know how to do a lot of things. Think about it. What do you do every day?" Natalya asked.

Elena was surprised. "I don't know. Just the usual things. I take care of the kids, clean the house, and do the laundry. I plan meals and go to the supermarket, and of course I cook."

"And you cook really well. What else do you do?"

"Nothing much. I sew, or work in the vegetable garden," Elena answered.

"See? You have *lots* of job skills," Natalya said. "You don't need certificates or papers. You have life experience!"

3. **Work in pairs. Complete the list of job skills for Elena.**

Present Job Title	Training	Job Skills
Homemaker	Life experience	Child care General cleaning

Reading and Writing

4. **What can you say about Binh?**

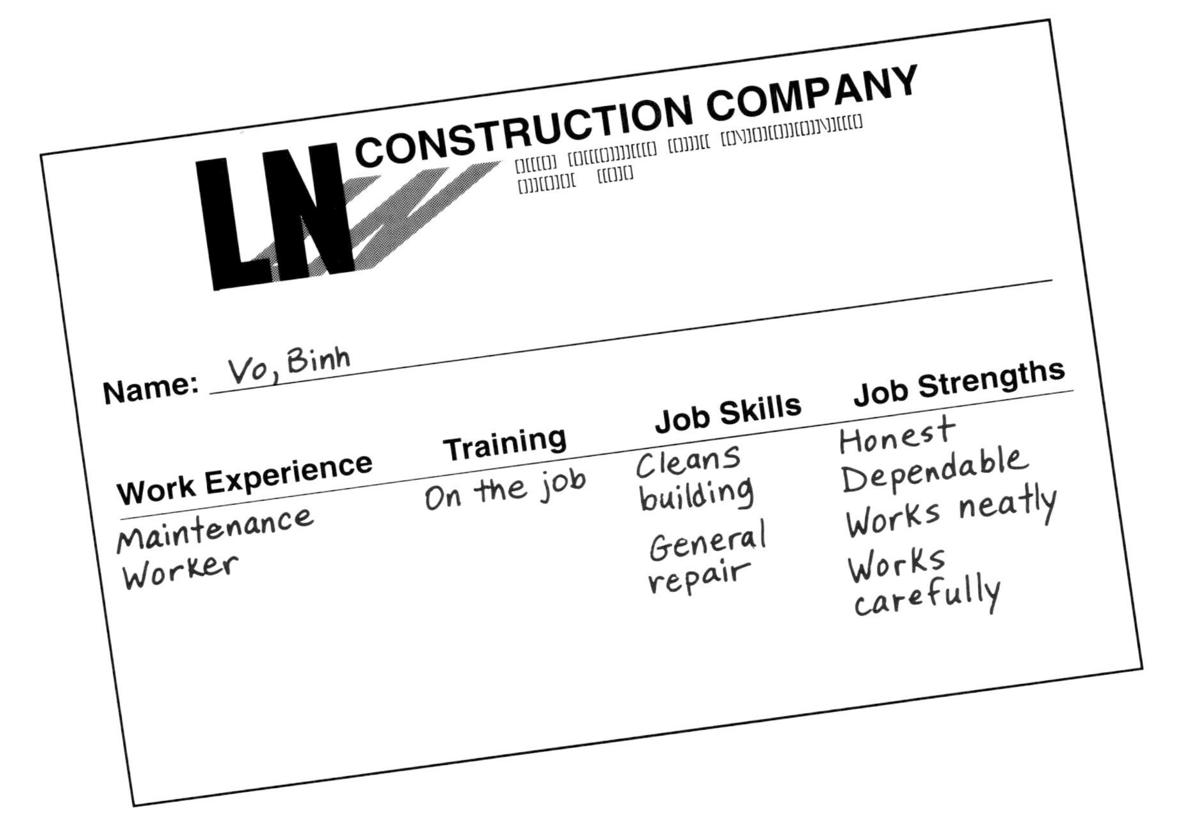

5. **Work in a group. List all the job strengths you know.**

dependable ________ ________ ________

________ ________ ________

________ ________ ________

________ ________ ________

e

6. **Work with a classmate. Talk about your work experience, training, job skills, and job strengths.**

7. **Make a chart of your work experience, training, job skills, and job strengths. Use the example in 4.**

8. **Read your chart to your group.**

9. **What has surprised you about working in the U.S.? Write about it.**

Listening Plus

1. Notice the difference.
Point.
Listen and write the sentences.

You see...	*but you hear...*
...can...	...*k'n*...
...can't...	...*kan(t)*...

a. ______________________________

b. ______________________________

2. Point.
Check.

PERSONNEL

JOB SKILLS	EDUCATION AND TRAINING
___ Drive a truck	___ Elementary school
___ General office skills	✓ High school
___ Use a cash register	___ College
___ Do basic alterations	___ Technical school
___ Operate a computer	___ On-the-job training
___ Operate a power sewing machine	___ Other
___ Work with children	

3. Fill in the information.

	Last Job	*From/To*	*Wages*
Charles	cook		
Roberta			
Willis			

4. What about you?

____

Interactions
Student A

1. Get information. Ask about the missing information on Kenji's application. Fill in the blanks.

A: What's Kenji's address ?
B: 8372 Lincoln Street, Apartment 2 .
A: Could you spell Lincoln, please ?
B: L-I-N-C-O-L-N .

APPLICATION FOR EMPLOYMENT

Name Asano (Last) Kenji (First) — (Middle)

Address 8372 (No.) Lincoln Street, Apt. 2 (Street) Bridgeton, (City) CA (State) 93202 (ZIP)

Phone No. (209) 571-3449 Soc. Sec. No. ___ - ___ - ___

Are you legally able to work in the U.S.? Yes X No ___

Are you 18 years or older? Yes ___ No ___ Position desired Waiter

Employment History

Dates of Employment	Name and Address of Company	Job Title	Job Duties	Salary
From Mo. Yr./To Mo. Yr. 6/91- Present		Waiter		$4.25
	Healthy Harvest Restaurant 679 12th Ave. Bridgeton, CA 93204		Clear tables	

Education and Training

School	Name and Location	No. of Years	Subjects	Date of Graduation
High School	Toshima Gakuen SHS Tokyo, Japan	3	General	
College	—			
Other	Westside Community Adult School Bridgeton, CA		English	—

I declare that the above information is true and correct to the best of my knowledge.

Signature: Kenji Asano Date: 3/21/93

2. Give information about Kenji's application.

3. Find out about getting a job in your partner's country.

Interactions

Student B

1. **Give information about Kenji's application.**

A: What's Kenji's address?
B: 8372 Lincoln Street, Apartment 2.
A: Could you spell Lincoln, please?
B: L-I-N-C-O-L-N.

APPLICATION FOR EMPLOYMENT

Name: Asano (Last) Kenji (First) — (Middle)

Address: 8372 (No.) Lincoln Street, Apt. 2 (Street) Bridgeton (City), CA (State) (ZIP)

Phone No. ( ) Soc. Sec. No. 373-43-9921

Are you legally able to work in the U.S.? Yes X No ___

Are you 18 years or older? Yes X No ___ Position desired ___

Employment History

Dates of Employment From Mo. Yr./To Mo. Yr.	Name and Address of Company	Job Title	Job Duties	Salary
	Union Street Restaurant 1275 Union St., Bridgeton, CA 93202		Serve food	
1/89-6/91		Busperson		$3.35

Education and Training

School	Name and Location	No. of Years	Subjects	Date of Graduation
High School	Toshima Gakuen SHS Tokyo, Japan		General	March, 1988
College	—			
Other	Westside Community Adult School Bridgeton, CA			—

I declare that the above information is true and correct to the best of my knowledge.

Signature: Kenji Asano Date: 3/21/93

2. **Get information. Ask about the missing information on Kenji's application. Fill in the blanks.**

3. **Find out about getting a job in your partner's country.**

Progress Checks

1. **c** ☐ Fill in a job application form.

Fill in this form.

EMPLOYMENT APPLICATION

Name ____
Last First MI

Address ____

____

Phone No. (   ) ____________ Soc. Sec. No. ____ – ____ – ____

Are you legally able to work in the U.S.? Yes ____ No ____

Are you 18 years or older? Yes ____ No ____ Position desired ____________

Employment History

Employer Name and Address	From/To	Position	Salary	Job Duties

Education and Training

School	Place	No. of Years	Subjects	Date of Graduation

I declare that the above information is true and correct to the best of my knowledge.

Signature: ______________________________ Date: ____________

Progress Checks

2. a ☐ Begin an interview appropriately.
   d ☐ Answer questions about your educational background.
   e ☐ Describe your work experience, training, job skills, and job strengths.
   b ☐ End an interview appropriately.

What are the people saying?

Do it yourself.

Problem Solving

John needs to hire a new delivery person for his pizza restaurant. Here are the applicants. Who should John hire? Why?

NAME	EXPERIENCE	DRIVING RECORD
Tony Romero →	Moe's Messengers, 3 months Burgers To Go, 6 months Left last job because he wanted more money →	1 parking ticket
Fred Remington →	Texas Taxis, 8 years → Amber Cab, 12 years Left last job because the company closed	2 accidents
Keo Savang →	No work experience, but loves to drive → Level 2 ESL student at Westside Adult School	perfect

Now role play.

UNIT

8 On the Job

Getting Started

1. Guess. Where are Yolanda and Diane? What are they doing? What are they saying?

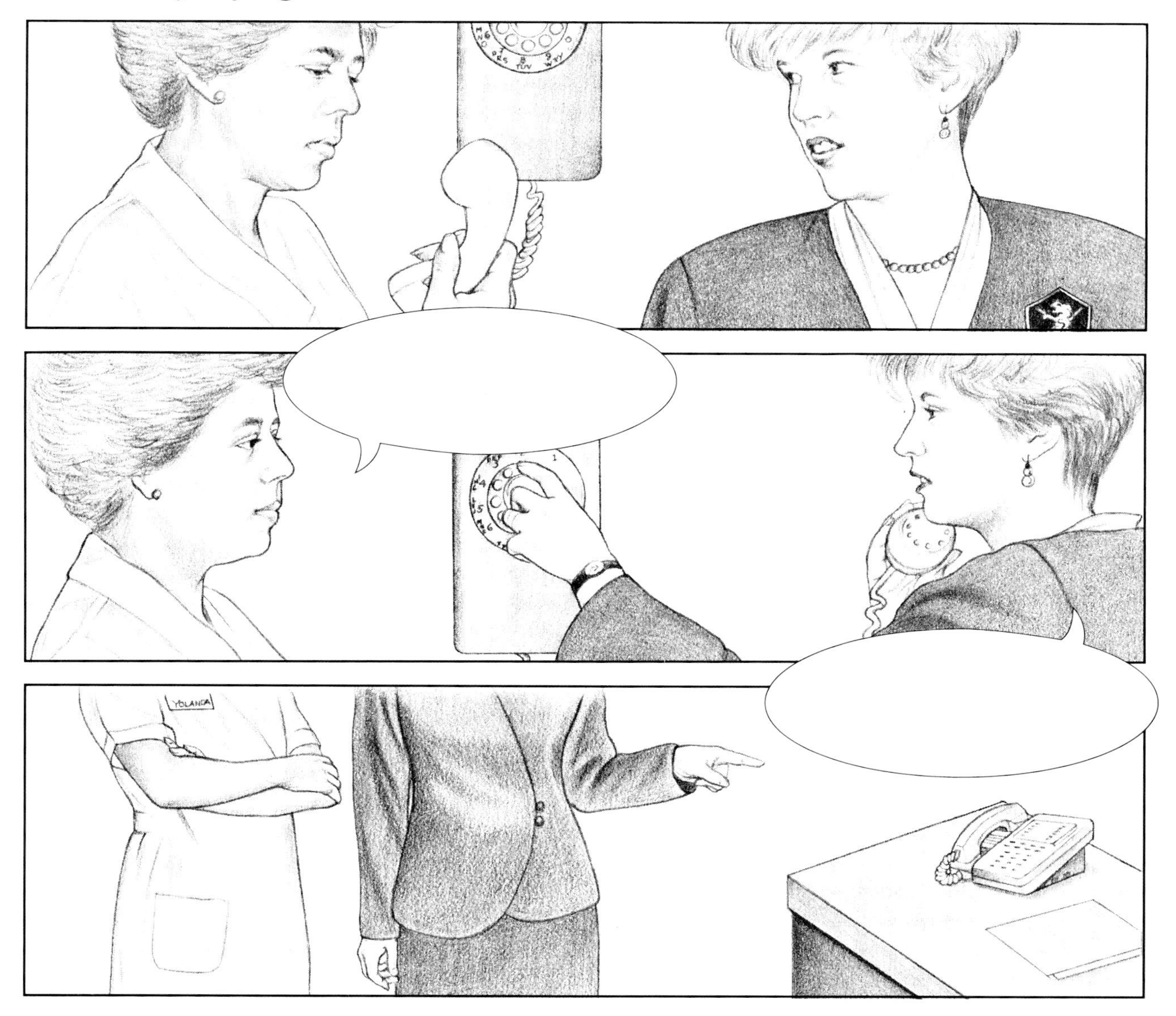

2. What can you hear?

Conversations

1. Practice.

Yolanda: Diane, I have a problem. This telephone isn't working.
Diane: Here. Let me see it.
Yolanda: Can you fix it?
Diane: I'm not sure. But in the meantime, you can use this one.
Yolanda: Thanks a lot.

2. What can you say? Add other words you know.

The computer isn't working.

The vacuum cleaner is making a strange noise.

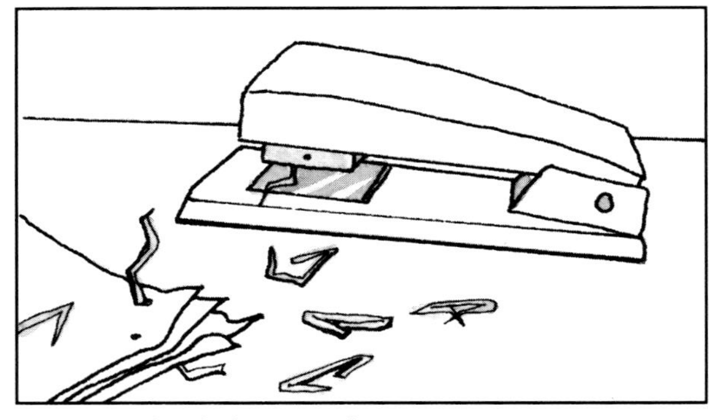

The stapler is jammed.

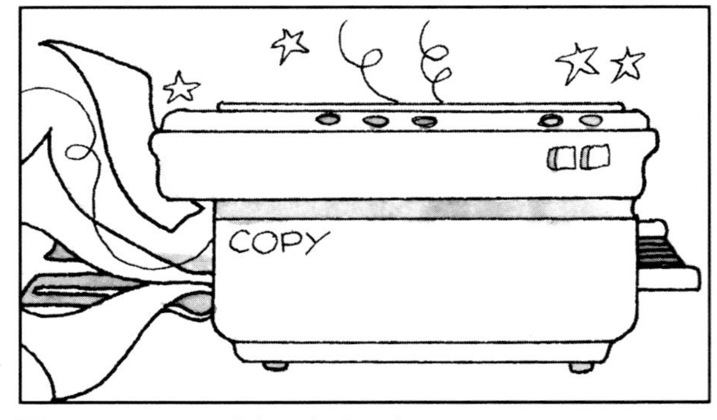

The copy machine is broken.

3. Ask for help with equipment at work. Use the conversation in 1 and the problems in 2.

4. Practice.

Yolanda: This phone is different from that one. What do I do?
Diane: Oh. Just push this button.
Yolanda: Which one? The first one or the second one?
Diane: The second one. Then dial 9 and wait for a dial tone.
Yolanda: I'm sorry. What was the last thing you said?
Diane: Dial 9 and wait for a dial tone.
Yolanda: OK. Thanks.

Conversations

5. Focus on grammar.

Which one? The blue one or the red one? The red one.	Which ones? The old ones or the new ones? The old ones.

6. Give instructions and ask for clarification.

A: Please take the envelopes to Room 214.
B: Which ones? The gray ones or the white ones?
A: The gray ones.

a. take the envelopes to Room 214
the gray/white envelopes

b. fix the tape recorder
the old/new tape recorder

c. press the button
the first/second button

d. put the boxes on the shelf
the large/small boxes

7. What can you say?

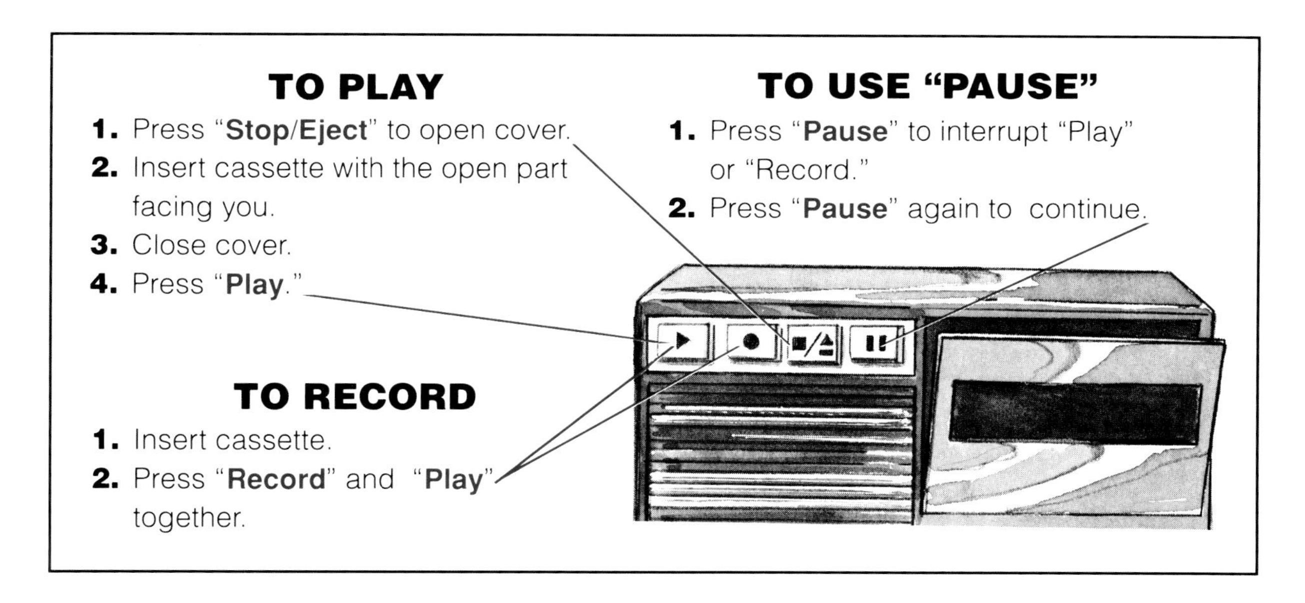

8. A, give B instructions. Tell B how to operate the tape recorder in 7. B, ask questions about anything you don't understand.

b
c

9. A, give B instructions. For example, tell B how to fill a stapler. B, ask questions about anything you don't understand.

Conversations

10. Practice.

Mrs. Kelly: Yolanda, can I see you, please?
Yolanda: Sure, Mrs. Kelly.
Mrs. Kelly: The guests in Room 335 called. You didn't leave clean towels.
Yolanda: 335? Oh, I'm sorry. I thought I did. I'll do it right away.
Mrs. Kelly: OK. And Yolanda, please be more careful.
Yolanda: Yes, Mrs. Kelly.

11. What can you say?

You forgot to connect these wires.
OK. I'll do it right away.

You used the wrong size screw.
Oh, I see. I won't do it again.

Your work is too slow.
I'll try to work faster.

This work is sloppy.
Sorry. I'll do it over.

12. Talk about problems at work. Use the words in 11.

A: ________________, can I see you, please?

B: Sure, ______________________________.

A: You forgot to connect these wires ______________________________.

B: OK. I'll do it right away ______________________________.

Paperwork

1. Read the check stub.

EMPLOYEE	PAY PERIOD	HOURLY WAGES	NO. OF HOURS THIS PAY PERIOD	GROSS WEEKLY EARNINGS
Garcia, Yolanda	6/19 – 6/26	$6.75	40	$270.00

F.I.C.A.	FEDERAL WH	STATE WH	TOTAL DEDUCTIONS	NET PAY
$20.25	$35.10	$5.40	$60.75	$209.25

e

2. Match.

F.I.C.A.	Take-home pay
Gross Weekly Earnings	U.S. tax
Federal WH	Social Security deduction
Net Pay	State tax
State WH	Pay before deductions
Pay Period	9/23–9/30

3. Add questions with your classmates. Then interview three classmates.

How often are you paid? every two weeks

Are you paid in cash or by check? by check

What items are deducted from your pay? Federal, state, and Social Security taxes.

_______________________________?

4. Pool your information. Then write summary sentences.

Reading and Writing

1. **What can you say about Ibrahim Tegri?**

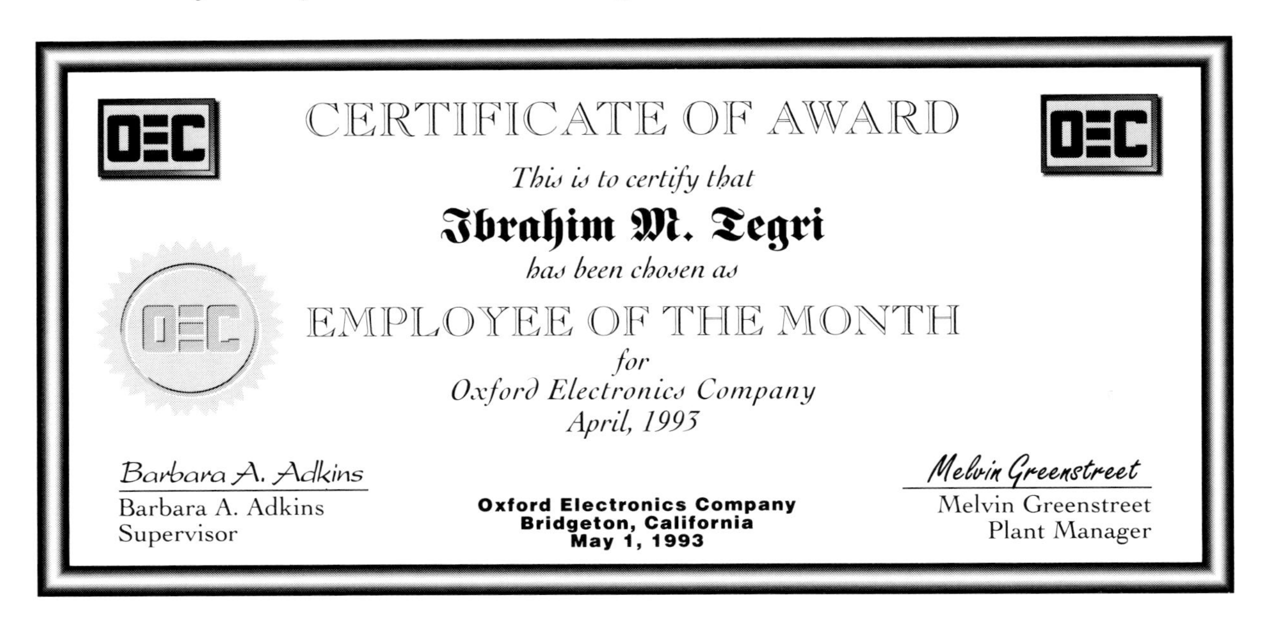

CERTIFICATE OF AWARD

This is to certify that

Ibrahim M. Tegri

has been chosen as

EMPLOYEE OF THE MONTH

for

Oxford Electronics Company

April, 1993

Barbara A. Adkins
Barbara A. Adkins
Supervisor

Oxford Electronics Company
Bridgeton, California
May 1, 1993

Melvin Greenstreet
Melvin Greenstreet
Plant Manager

2. **Read about Ibrahim. Circle a word you want to learn. Work with your classmates. Find out what it means.**

Oxford Electronics Company *NEWS*

MAY 1993 **VOLUME III, ISSUE 5**

IBRAHIM TEGRI—EMPLOYEE OF THE MONTH

Our Employee of the Month for April is **Ibrahim Tegri**. Tegri is an electronics assembly worker at our Bridgeton plant. He joined Oxford Electronics 18 months ago.

Plant Manager **Mel Greenstreet** speaks highly of Tegri. "Tegri does quality work," says Greenstreet. "He has an outstanding performance record with Oxford." Greenstreet says that Tegri is a hard worker—he always gets to work on time, he works quickly, and he follows instructions carefully.

Barbara Adkins, Tegri's line supervisor, says that he is very popular on the line. "Ibrahim is always cheerful and cooperative, and he really works well with his co-workers," says Adkins.

"Oxford Electronics is a great place to work," says Tegri. "I'm very proud to be Employee of the Month."

3. **Work with a partner. Why was Ibrahim chosen to be Employee of the Month? Underline all the reasons in 2.**

Reading and Writing

4. **What can you say about the evaluation report?**

SEMI-ANNUAL EMPLOYEE EVALUATION REPORT

Date: ____________

Employee: ____________________ **Job Title:** ____________________________

1 = Always **2 = Usually** **3 = Sometimes** **4 = Never**

Attendance				
a. Is on time for work	1	2	3	4
b. Calls in if unable to come to work	1	2	3	4
Work Habits				
a. Hard-working, quick	1	2	3	4
b. Takes good care of tools/equipment	1	2	3	4
Dependability				
a. Finishes work on time	1	2	3	4
b. Follows instructions thoroughly	1	2	3	4
Cooperation				
a. Works well with others	1	2	3	4
b. Takes criticism well	1	2	3	4

5. **What kind of worker or student are you? Circle the numbers for yourself. Then compare your form to your partner's.**

6. **Choose one of your classmates to be Student of the Month. Write about him or her. Use the article in 2 and the words in 4.**

7. **Read your article to your group.**

8. **What has surprised you about workers in the U.S.? Write about it.**

Listening Plus

1. Notice the difference.
Point.
Listen and write the sentences.

You see...	***but you hear...***
...him...	*...'im...*
...her...	*...'er...*

a. ______________________________

b. ______________________________

2. Point.
Circle.

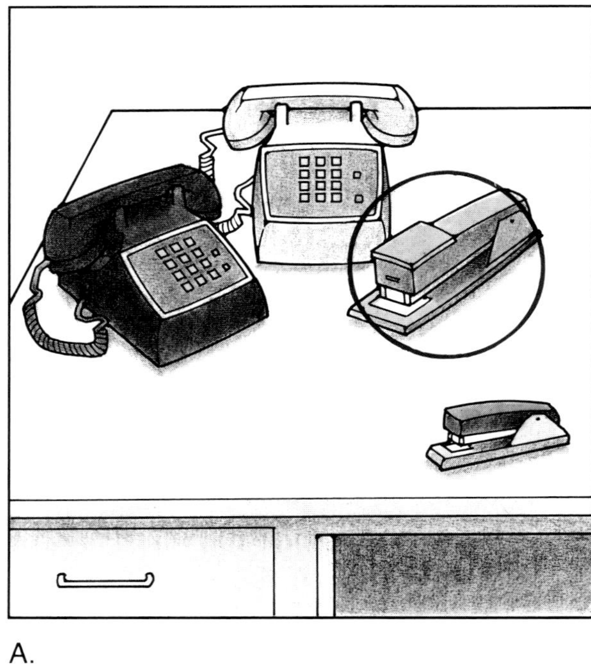

A.

B.

3. Fill in the information.

	Job Duty	***Problem***
Marie	make copies	
Oscar		
Rosalie		

4. What about you?

____

Interactions

Student A

f

1. Give instructions.

A: In the first square, first,

draw a line from 1 to 7.

Next, draw a line from 7 to 5.

Next, draw a line from 5 to 9.

Last, draw a line from 9 to 3.

What letter did you draw?

B: W.

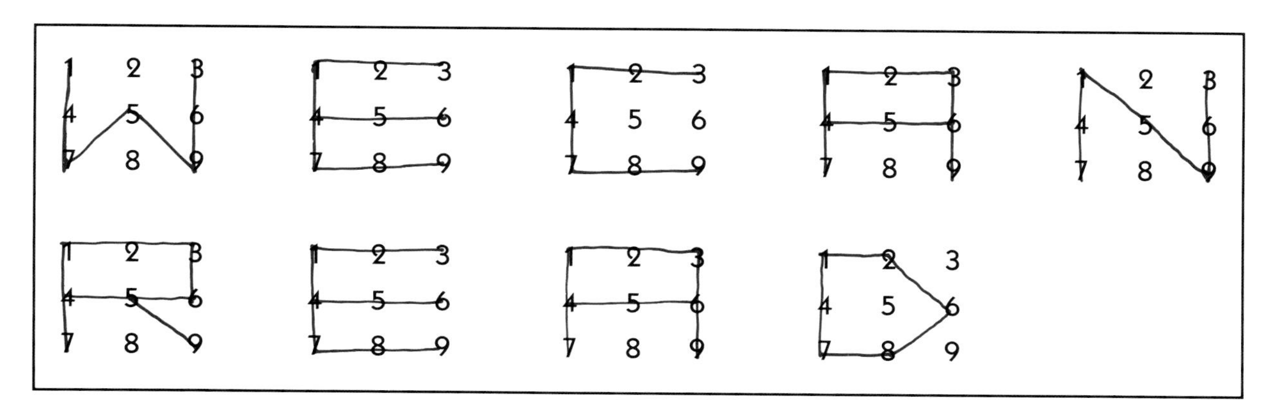

2. Get instructions.

1	2	3	1	2	3	1	2	3	1	2	3	1	2	3
4	5	6	4	5	6	4	5	6	4	5	6	4	5	6
7	8	9	7	8	9	7	8	9	7	8	9	7	8	9
1	2	3	1	2	3	1	2	3	1	2	3	1	2	3
4	5	6	4	5	6	4	5	6	4	5	6	4	5	6
7	8	9	7	8	9	7	8	9	7	8	9	7	8	9

3. Work with your partner. Put your words together and write the sentence.

4. Find out about paycheck deductions in your partner's country.

Interactions

Student B

1. Get instructions.

A: In the first square, first,
draw a line from 1 to 7.
Next, draw a line from 7 to 5.
Next, draw a line from 5 to 9.
Last, draw a line from 9 to 3.
What letter did you draw?

B: W.

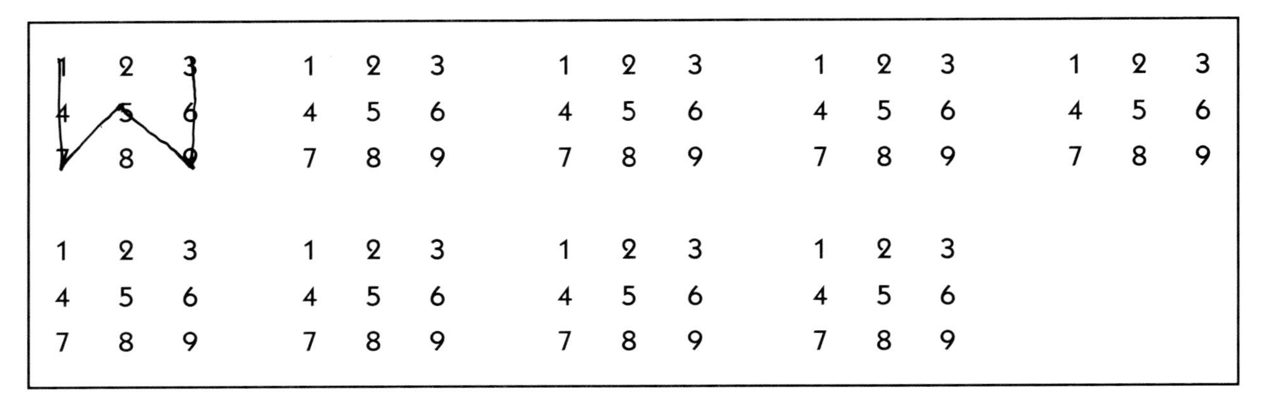

f

2. Give instructions.

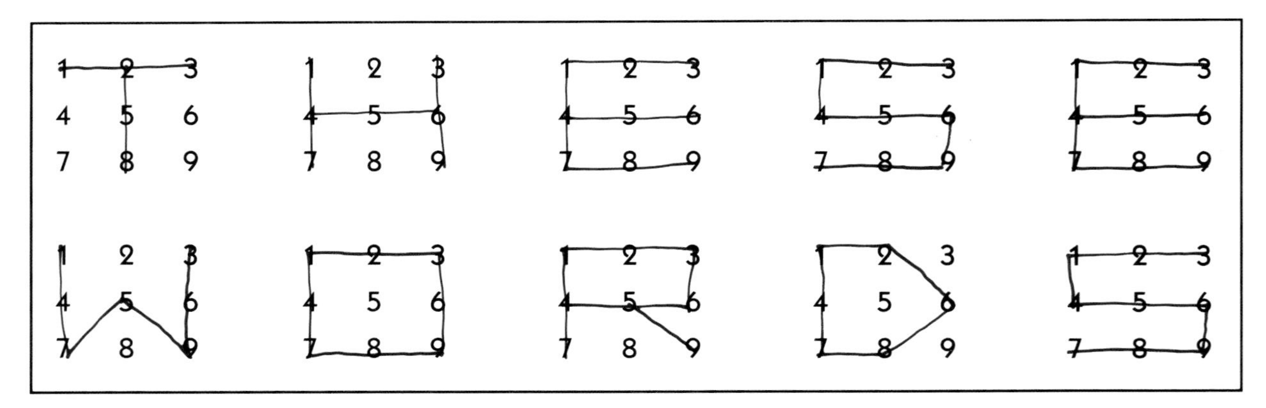

3. Work with your partner. Put your words together and write the sentence.

4. Find out about paycheck deductions in your partner's country.

Progress Checks

1. e ☐ Read a paycheck stub.

EMPLOYEE	PAY PERIOD	HOURLY WAGES	NO. OF HOURS THIS PAY PERIOD	GROSS WEEKLY EARNINGS
Baker, Ralph	5/11–5/18	$5.25	37.5	$196.88

F.I.C.A.	FEDERAL WH	STATE WH	TOTAL DEDUCTIONS	NET PAY
$14.77	$25.59	$3.94	$44.30	$152.58

a. How much is the deduction for Social Security taxes? ____________

b. How much is the deduction for U.S. taxes? ____________

c. What is Ralph Baker's take-home pay this pay period? ____________

2. b ☐ Briefly explain how to work a simple piece of equipment.
c ☐ Identify which part of instructions you did not understand.

A, choose Play, Record, or Pause and tell B how to do it. B, follow directions. Ask questions about anything you don't understand.

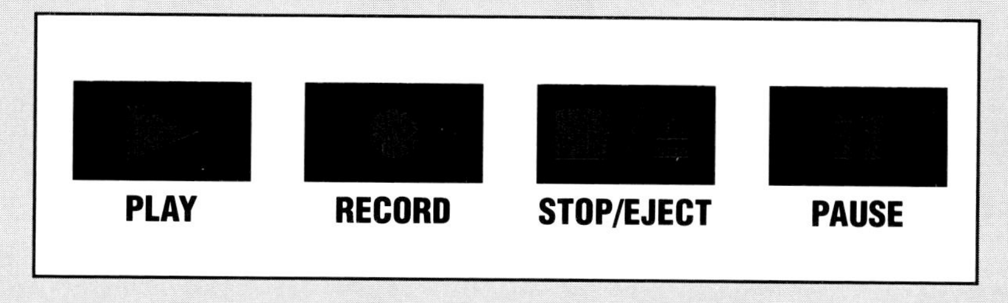

3. f ☐ Tell someone how to do a routine task, giving step-by-step verbal instructions.

A, pick a four-letter word and give your partner instructions to write the word. B, follow the instructions.

a	b	c		a	b	c		a	b	c		a	b	c
d	e	f		d	e	f		d	e	f		d	e	f
g	h	i		g	h	i		g	h	i		g	h	i

Progress Checks

4. **d** ☐ Respond to a supervisor's comments about the quality of your work.
   a ☐ Report specific problems found in completing a task.

What are the people saying?

Do it yourself.

Problem Solving

What's Chang's problem?

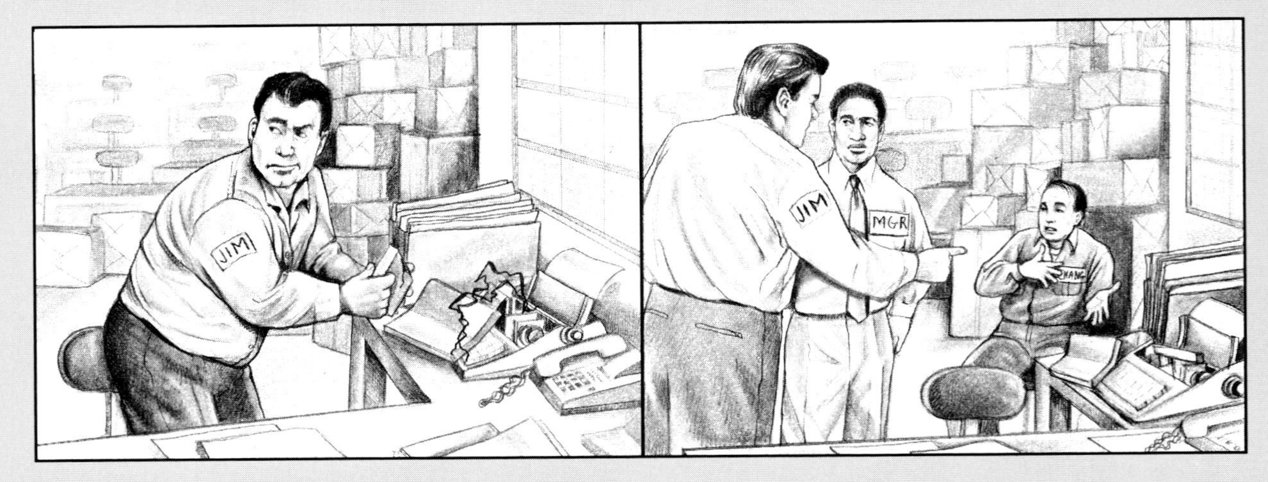

What should Chang do?
Now role play.

UNIT

9 Recreation

Getting Started

1. **Guess. Where are An Ling and Arturo? What are they doing? What are they saying?**

2. **What can you hear?**

Conversations

1. Practice.

An Ling: What are you doing this weekend, Arturo?
Arturo: Well, on Saturday, I'm painting the kitchen. On Sunday, I'm having a barbecue for some friends.
An Ling: Hey, that's great!
Arturo: I'm really looking forward to it. I hope the weather is good. And then on Monday, I'm going fishing.
An Ling: On Monday?
Arturo: Yes. It's a holiday. I have the day off.
An Ling: Lucky you! I'm working. But on Sunday afternoon, I'm playing volleyball, and on Sunday evening, I'm going to the movies.

2. What can you say? Add other words you know.

having a barbecue

going fishing

playing volleyball

3. Focus on grammar.

What	are they	doing	on Monday?
	is An Ling		tomorrow?

She's / We're	(not)	having a barbecue. / going fishing.

4. Add words. Talk about your weekend plans.

go bowling　　have a party　　________

________　　________　　________

A: What are you doing this weekend.
B: I'm going bowling. What about you?
A: ________________.

Conversations

5. Practice.

Arturo: What movie are you seeing, An Ling?
An Ling: *Rocky VI.* I'm taking the children.
Arturo: You are? I saw it. You know, it's the most violent of all the *Rocky* movies.
An Ling: Really? I didn't know that. Maybe we should go to another movie.
Arturo: Maybe. But it's also the most exciting one.

6. What can you say?

violent

exciting

frightening

romantic

entertaining

boring

7. Focus on grammar.

violent	the most violent
interesting	interesting
boring	boring

8. Talk about movies or TV shows you know. Use the words in 6.

A: What movie ______ do you think is the most romantic ______?

B: Casablanca ______. I think it's the most romantic ______ of all.

What about you?

A: ______________________________

Conversations

9. Practice.

An Ling: By the way, Arturo, what's the holiday on Monday?
Arturo: Memorial Day.
An Ling: What's that?
Arturo: It's the day people remember dead soldiers.
An Ling: Oh. We have a day like that in Korea.

10. What can you say? Add other holidays in the U.S.

New Year's Eve
people celebrate
the new year

Valentine's Day
people remember
their sweethearts

Mother's Day
people remember
their mothers

Memorial Day
people remember
dead soldiers

Halloween
children dress in costumes
and go trick-or-treating

Thanksgiving
people give thanks

11. Talk about the holidays in 10.

A: What is Memorial Day?

B: It's the day people remember dead soldiers.

A: What do people do?

B: They visit the cemetery.

Paperwork

1. Read the weather map.

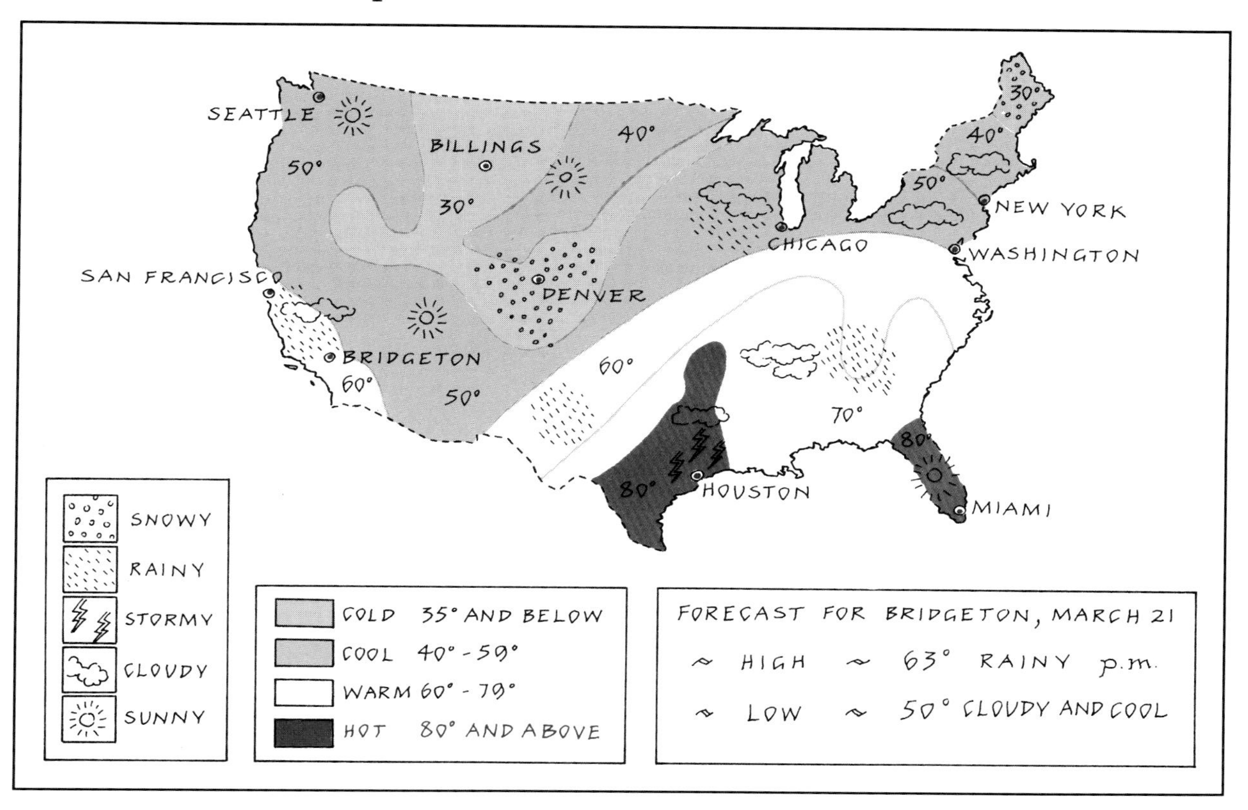

d

2. Answer.

a. What's the weather forecast for Bridgeton today? ____________

b. Where will it be hot and stormy? ____________

c. Where will it be cool and sunny? ____________

d. Where will it be cold and snowy? ____________

e. How's the weather where you are right now? ____________

e

3. Add questions with your classmates. Then interview three classmates.

How's the weather in your country in May? warm

How's the weather in your country in December? cold and rainy

What kind of weather do you like? warm and sunny

____________?

4. Pool your information. Then write summary sentences.

Reading and Writing

1. What can you say about Bridgeton's Fourth of July celebration?

2. Read the newspaper article about July 4th in Bridgeton. Circle a word you want to learn. Work with your classmates. Find out what it means.

July 4th — America's Birthday Party

What's your favorite way to celebrate the Fourth of July? We talked to three Bridgeton families who are planning to enjoy their holiday weekend in traditional American ways.

Polly and Joe Johnson are taking their kids to the big parade downtown. "We love the marching bands, the flags, and the color," Polly told us. "It's a real American celebration."

George and Elsie Wilson are going to their annual family reunion at Westside Park. They'll have hotdogs, corn on the cob, and, of course, watermelon. Their sons, Mark, 10, and Tony, 12, are getting ready for the three-legged race.

"We're all going to the stadium to see the Bears," Mercurio Estevantes said. "Baseball. That's what July 4th means in our family."

The Chamber of Commerce promises the most dazzling fireworks display in Bridgeton history. It's free, and it all starts at dusk at Miller Stadium. See you there! Happy birthday, America!

3. Work with a partner. List the activities in 2 in the following columns. (Some activities can go in more than one column.)

Things to Hear	*Things to See*	*Things to Taste*	*Things to Smell*	*Things to Do*
______	______	______	______	______
______	______	______	______	______
______	______	______	______	______
______	______	______	______	______

Reading and Writing

4. **What can you say about the pictures and notes?**

January 22

Dear Mom,

We hope you had a nice time on Martin Luther King Day. Jack and the kids and I went to hear speeches and see videos of Dr. King. The choir sang some magnificent hymns. It was a beautiful program.

Love,
Lucy

Dear Elizabeth, December 18

Merry Christmas! Here's a picture of our family in front of the tree. Isn't it big? I still have to buy a few more presents to put under it. We're having all of Bill's family here for dinner on Christmas Eve.

Have a happy holiday and a prosperous new year.

Jean

5. **Work with a classmate. Talk about what you do on different holidays.**

6. **Write a note to a friend about a holiday. Use your imagination. Use the notes in 4 as examples.**

7. **Read your note to your group.**

8. **What has surprised you about holidays in the U.S.? Write about it.**

Listening Plus

1. Notice the difference.
Point.
Listen and write the sentences.

You see...	***but you hear...***
What are you...?	*Whaddaya...?*
Where are you...?	*Where 're ya...?*

a. ______________________

b. ______________________

2. Point.
Number.

3. Fill in the information.

	December	***March***	***July***
Bridgeton			
Denver			
New York City		cool, rainy	

4. What about you?

____

Interactions

Student A

1. Ask B about the holidays, and write the activities in the correct box.

A: What do people do on Father's Day?

B: They give presents to their fathers.

A: They give...?

B: They give presents to their fathers.

New Year's Eve

Valentine's Day

Mother's Day

Memorial Day

Father's Day

People give presents to their fathers.

Independence Day

Halloween

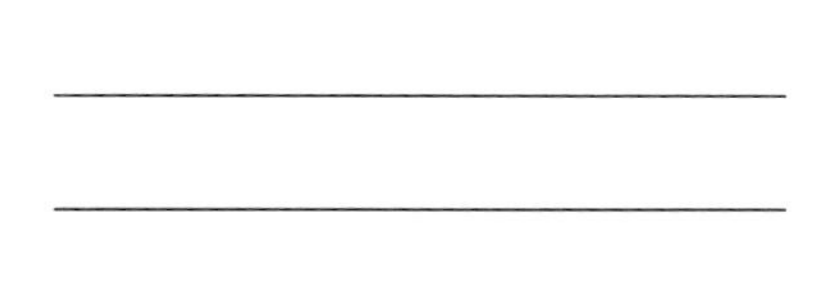

Christmas

Thanksgiving

2. Look at the picture and tell B what people do on the holiday.

f

3. Find out about holidays in your partner's country.

Interactions

Student B

1. Look at the picture and tell A what people do on the holiday.

A: What do people do on Father's Day?

B: They give presents to their fathers.

A: They give...?

B: They give presents to their fathers.

New Year's Eve

Valentine's Day

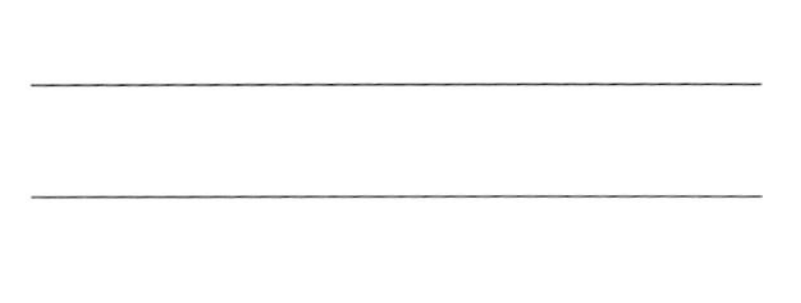

Mother's Day

Memorial Day

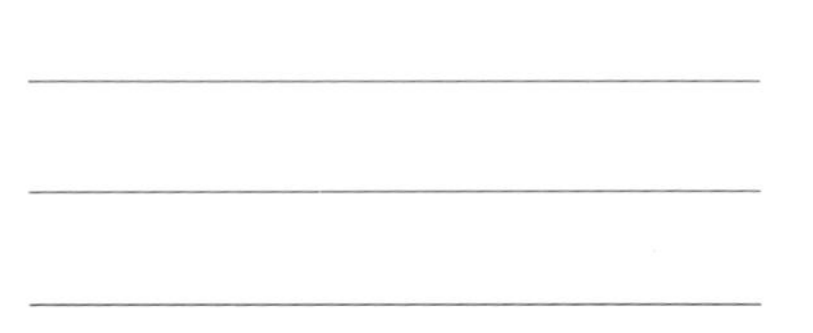

Father's Day

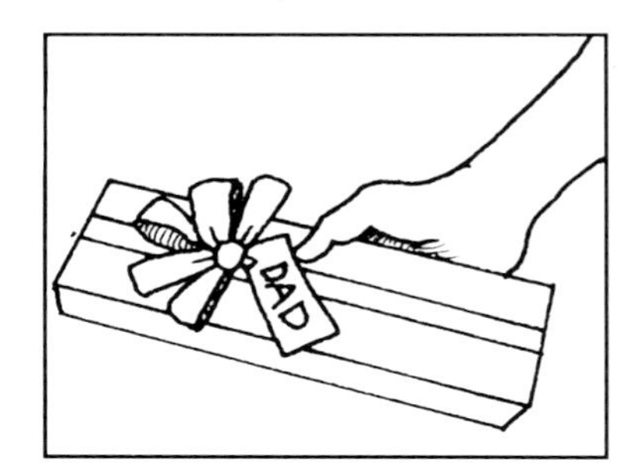

Independence Day

Halloween

Christmas

Thanksgiving

2. Ask A about the holidays, and write the activities in the correct box.

f

3. Find out about holidays in your partner's country.

Progress Checks

1. **d** ☐ Read a weather map.

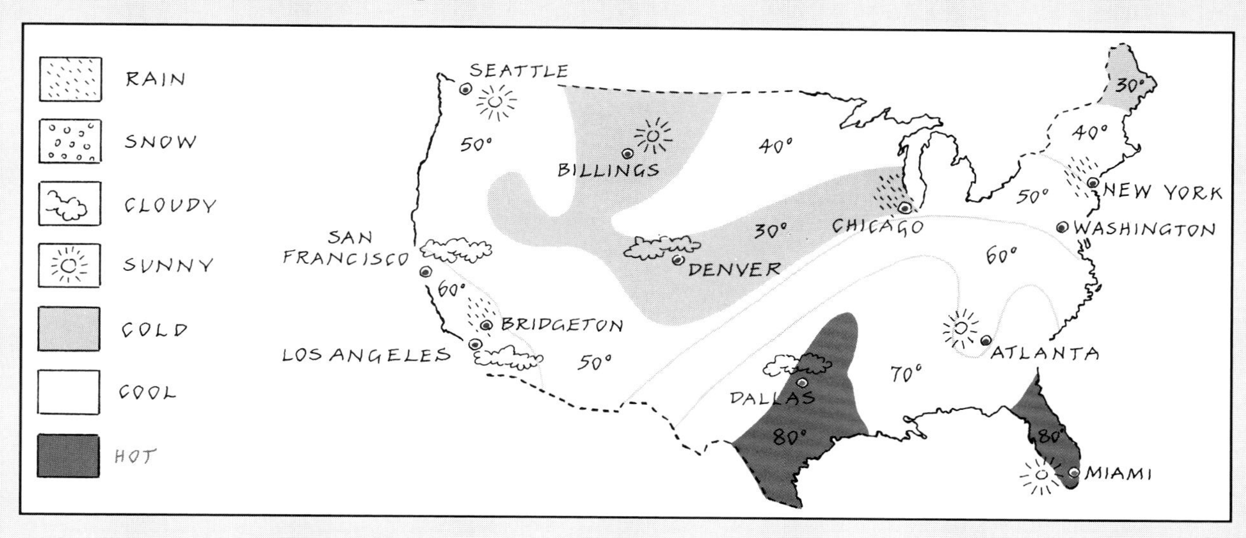

Answer these questions.

a. What's the weather forecast for Dallas?
b. Where will the weather be sunny and hot?

2. **e** ☐ Ask and answer questions about the weather.
a ☐ Ask and answer questions about weekend plans and recreation.

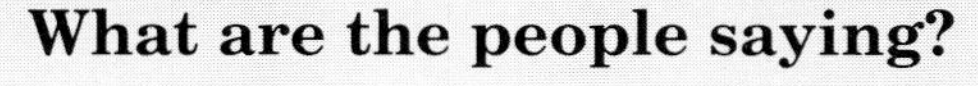

What are the people saying?

Do it yourself.

Progress Checks

3. **b** ☐ Identify major U.S. holidays.
   c ☐ Ask and answer questions about holidays in the U.S. and common ways to celebrate them.
   f ☐ Answer questions about holidays in your country of origin.

What are the people saying?

Do it yourself.

Problem Solving

What's Misha's problem?

What should Misha do?
Now role play.

UNIT 10 Transportation

Getting Started

1. **Guess. Where are Luisa, Ilona, and Kenji? What are they doing? What are they saying?**

2. **What can you hear?**

Conversations

1. Practice.

Ilona: What happened, Luisa?
Luisa: There was an accident. I was standing here when it happened.
Kenji: Did you see it?
Luisa: Yes. The white car was waiting at the light when the red car hit it.
Ilona: Is everyone all right?
Luisa: Yes, I think so.

2. Focus on grammar.

The white car	was	waiting at the light	when	the red car hit it.
They	were	standing at the bus stop		it happened.

3. Talk about the people.

A: What was he doing when the accident happened?
B: He was standing on the corner.

the accident happened

the plane took off

the car ran the red light

the bus broke down

Conversations

4. Practice.

Ilona: Are you taking a vacation, Luisa?
Luisa: Yes. Arturo, the kids, and I are driving home to visit our family.
Kenji: You're really lucky. You can drive to Mexico. I can't drive to Japan.
Luisa: Are you from a small town or a big city?
Kenji: I'm from Kyoto. It's a big city. What about you?
Luisa: I'm from a small town.

5. What can you say?

village

town

city

6. Talk about your hometown.

A: Are you from a small town or a big city?

B: I'm from Kyoto. It's a big city in Japan.

What about you?

A: I'm from Rio Grande. It's a small town in Mexico.

Conversations

7. Practice.

Man: Miss! Miss! Is this your umbrella?
Ilona: No, it isn't mine. Kenji, is it yours?
Kenji: No. I left mine at home. I think it's Luisa's umbrella. It looks like hers.
Ilona: I'll take it for her. Thank you.
Man: Sure. No problem.

8. Focus on grammar.

Whose						
Whose	book is this?	It's	her your our my their	book.	It's	hers. yours. ours. mine. theirs.
	books are these?	They're	his	books.	They're	his.

9. Talk about the things.

A: Whose keys are these?
B: They're not mine. I think they're Devi's keys.
They look like hers.

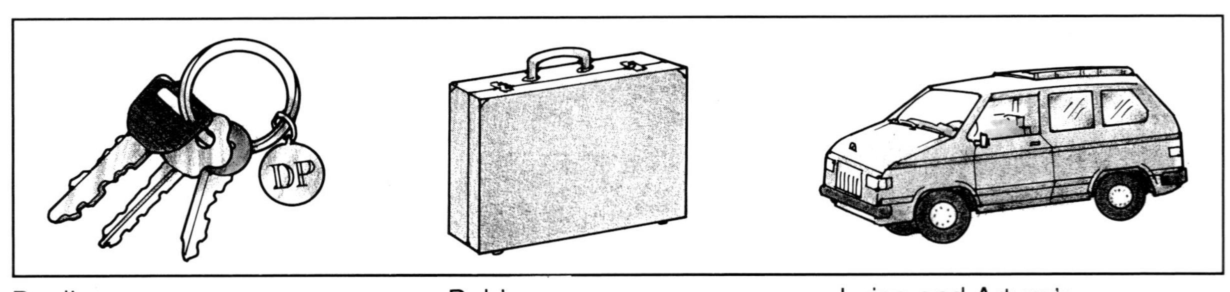

Devi's Bob's Luisa and Arturo's

Kenji's Reuben's and Binh's Yolanda's

Paperwork

1. Read the Bridgeton bus schedule.

BRIDGETON BUSWAYS **Departure Schedule: Route A**

Weekdays
6:30 a.m. – 9:30 a.m. — every 15 min.
9:37 a.m. – 4:07 p.m. — every 30 min.
4:15 p.m. – 7:00 p.m. — every 15 min.

Saturdays
10:00 a.m. – 5:00 p.m. — every 15 min.

Sundays
10:00 a.m. – 5:00 p.m. — every 30 min.

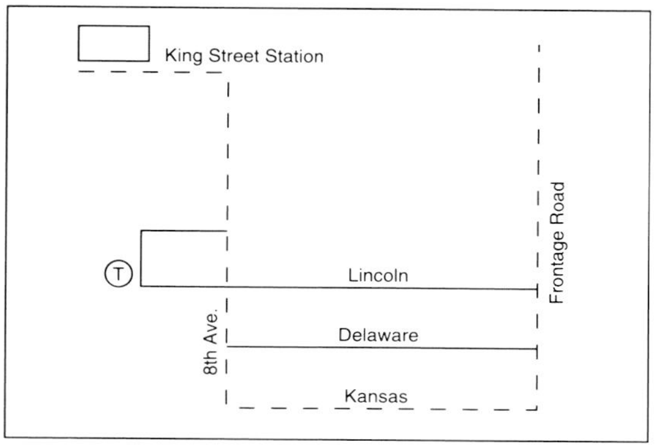

Weekday Schedule, Route A

Lv King St. Sta	Due Lincoln & 8 Av N	Due Delaware & 8 Av N	Due Kansas & Frontage
6:30 a.m.	6:44 a.m.	6:52 a.m.	7:10 a.m.
6:45	6:59	7:07	7:25
7:00	7:14	7:22	7:40
7:15	7:29	7:37	7:55

a

2. Answer.

Ilona works at the Valley View Restaurant. She has to take the bus to work. She catches the bus at Lincoln and 8th Avenue North. She gets off at the Kansas and Frontage stop. It takes ten minutes to walk from the bus stop to the restaurant, and she needs to be at work by 7:30 a.m. Which bus should Ilona take to get to work on time?

____

3. Add questions with your classmates. Then interview three classmates.

How do you usually get to school or work? by bus and walking

How long does the trip take? about 36 minutes

What does it cost every week? $7.50

______________________________?

4. Pool your information. Then write summary sentences.

Reading and Writing

1. What can you say about the bus fares in Bridgeton?

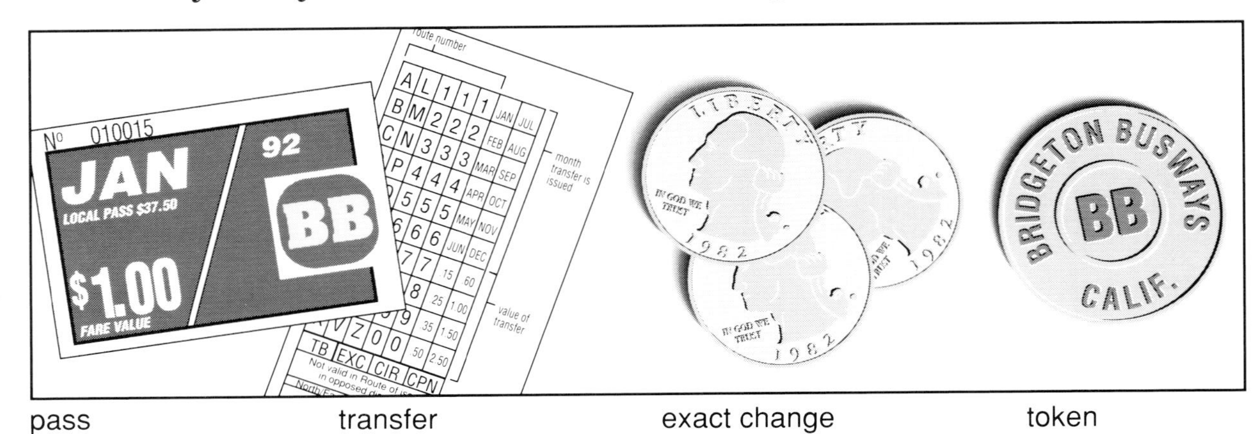

pass transfer exact change token

2. Read the information about Bridgeton Busways. Circle a word you want to learn. Work with your classmates. Find out what it means.

<u>Cost:</u> 75¢ will take you anywhere in Bridgeton. You must have exact change or tokens.

<u>Transfers:</u> For free transfer to another route, pick up a transfer as you board your bus. Give it to the driver of your connecting bus. Transfers are valid for a limited time. Transfer locations are marked with a T on schedules, route signs, and route maps.

<u>Passes:</u> For one discounted monthly price, you can travel as many times as you wish.

<u>Tokens and passes</u> are available at the Bridgeton Bus Station or at any Best in the West or Foodsmart Supermarket.

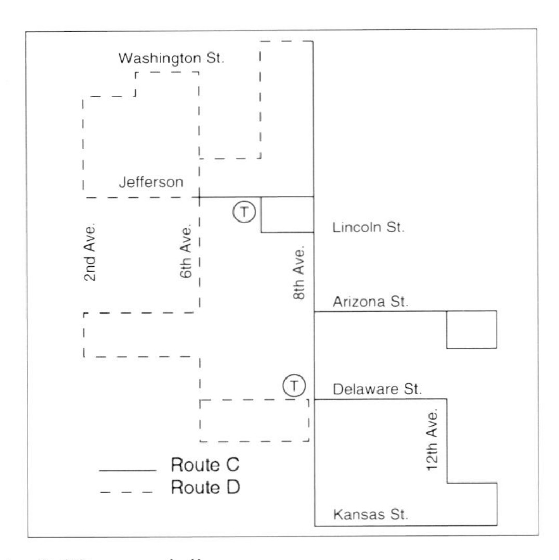

For more information, call 209-BUS-INFO, 6:00 a.m. to 6:00 p.m. daily.

3. Work in pairs. Answer these questions.

a. How much is the bus in Bridgeton?
b. You gave the driver $1.00. Will the driver give you change?
c. How many times can you ride the bus with a pass?
d. Where can you buy tokens or passes?
e. What number do you call for bus information?

Reading and Writing

4. **Read the map of Bridgeton.**

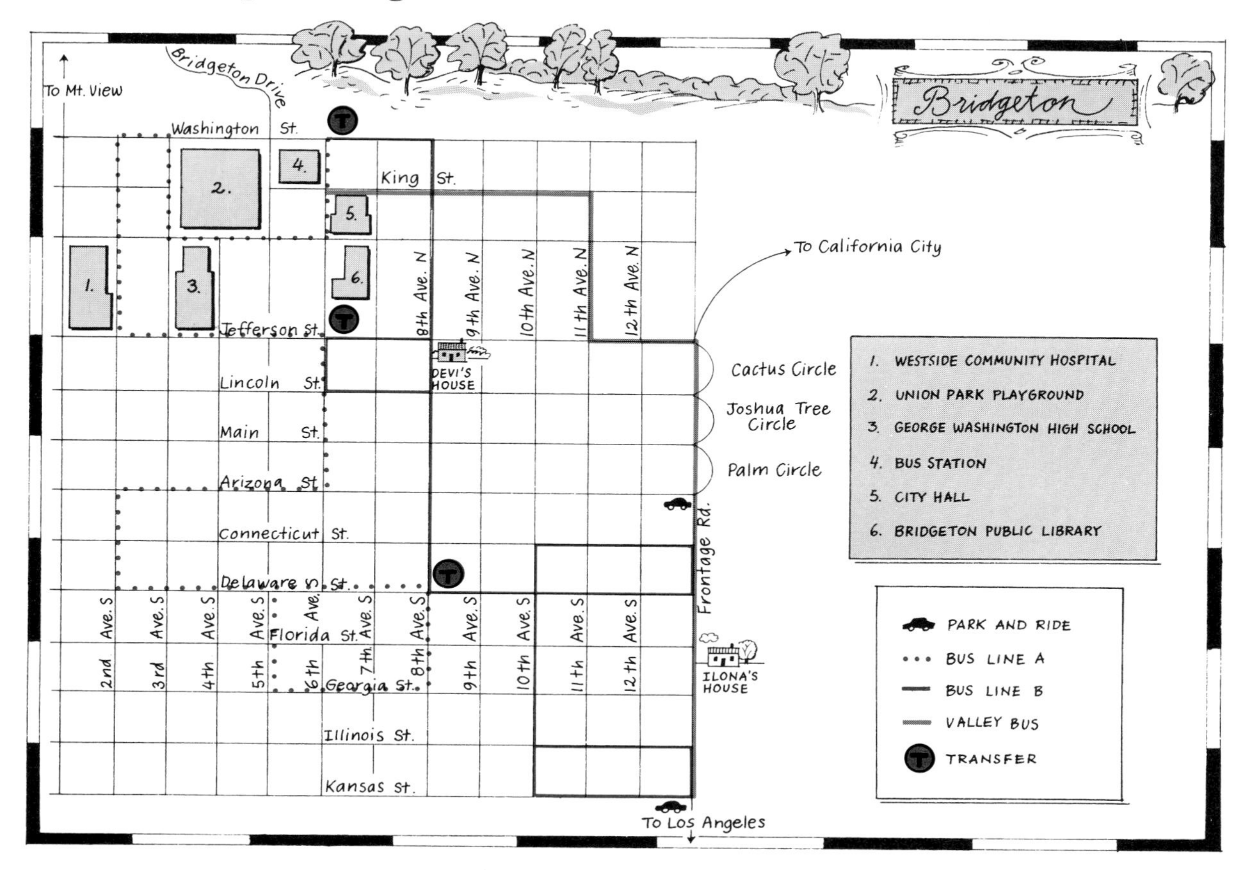

5. **Ilona gave Devi these directions to her house.**

> Go east on Lincoln to 11th Avenue.
> Turn right on 11th. Go south to Arizona.
> Turn left on Arizona. Go 2 blocks to Frontage Road. Turn right and go 1/2 mile south.
> My address is 3234 Frontage Road.
> It's the small, white house on the left.

b 6. **Follow Ilona's directions. Circle her house on the map in 4.**

c 7. **A, you are at Ilona's house. Write directions to a place in Bridgeton. Use the map in 4. Give the directions to B. B, find the places.**

8. **What has surprised you about transportation in the U.S.? Write about it.**

Listening Plus

1. **Notice the difference.**
   Point.
   Listen and write the sentences.

You see...	***but you hear...***
are you...?	*'er ya...?*
were you...?	*were ya...?*

a. ______________________________

b. ______________________________

2. **Point.**
   Number.

3. **Fill in the information.**

	Where to catch the bus	***What time to catch the bus***	***Where to get off the bus***
Kenji	Lincoln and 8th		
Yolanda			
Binh			

4. **What about you?**

____

Interactions

Student A

d

1. **Get directions. Ask B about places to go to. Where is B giving directions to? Write the activity next to the correct number in the legend below. Ask where you can:**

hike

camp

hunt

ride bikes

A: Where's a good place to hike?

B: Take Highway 36 to Martin Falls. Turn west on 119 and go straight.

A: Is that Kent? Is that #4 in the legend?

B: Yes.

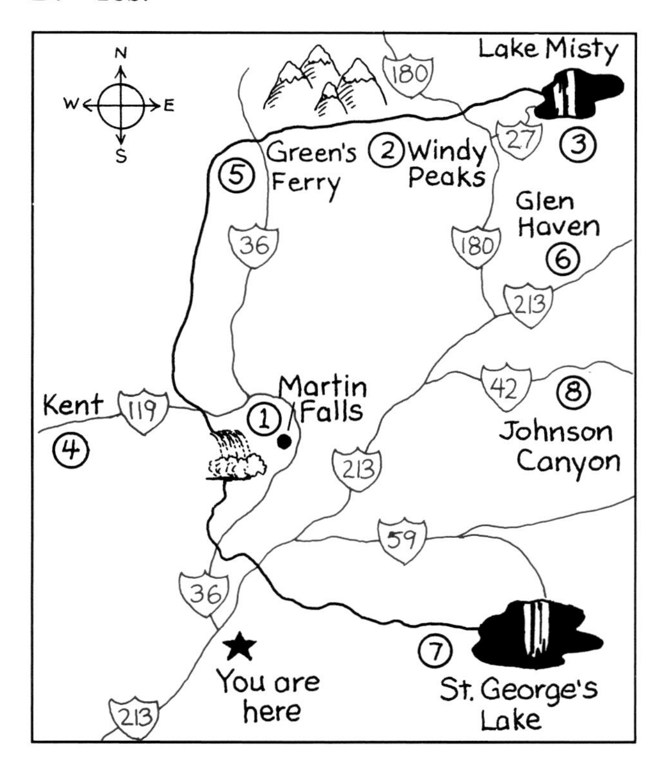

1. take pictures 2. ____________

3. picnic 4. hike

5. fish 6. ____________

7. swim 8. ____________

2. **Give directions. Look at the map and the legend. Find the place on the map that B wants to go to. Don't say the name of the final destination.**

3. **Find out about driving in your partner's country.**

Interactions

Student B

1. **Give directions. Look at the map and the legend. Find the place on the map that A wants to go to. Don't say the name of the final destination.**

A: Where's a good place to hike?

B: Take Highway 36 to Martin Falls. Turn west on 119 and go straight.

A: Is that Kent? Is that #4 in the legend?

B: Yes.

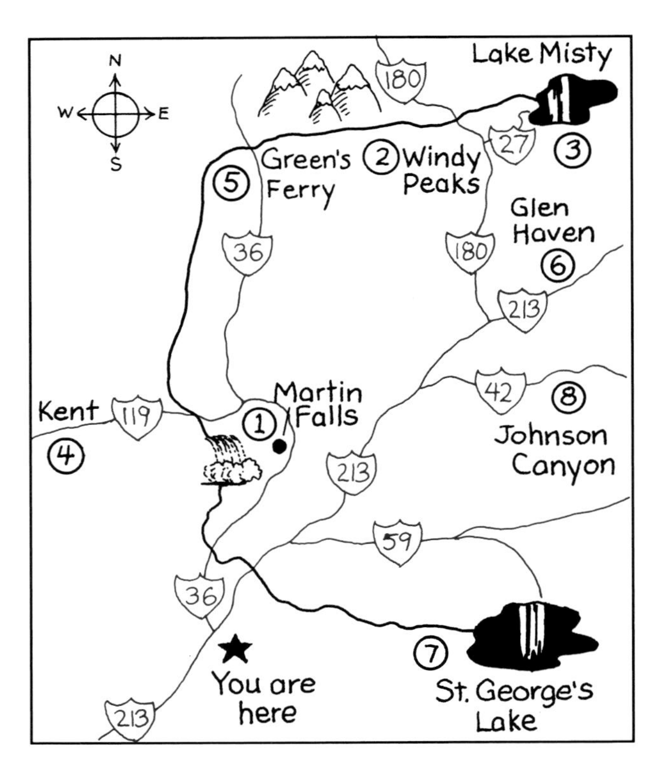

1. ______ 2. hunt

3. ______ 4. hike

5. ______ 6. ride bikes

7. ______ 8. camp

d

2. **Get directions. Ask A about places to go to. Where is A giving directions to? Write the activity next to the correct number in the legend below. Ask where you can:**

take pictures

picnic

fish

swim

3. **Find out about driving in your partner's country.**

Progress Checks

1. a ☐ Read a bus schedule.

Weekday Schedule, Red Route

Lv Central Bus Station	Broadway & C Street	Texas & F Street	New York & M Street
5:47 a.m.	6:01 a.m.	6:13 a.m.	6:28 a.m.
6:07	6:21	6:32	6:47
6:27	6:41	6:53	7:08
6:47	7:01	7:13	7:28

You are at Broadway and C Street. You want to go to New York and M Street. You need to be there at 7:00 a.m. What time do you catch the bus?

____

2. b ☐ Find a place by following simple written directions.
c ☐ Use a map to find a place.

Look at the map. Read the directions. Where will you meet Virginia? Circle the place on the map.

Please meet me at the park at about 3:30. Take the path on the left. Go past the volleyball court and the playground. Take the next path on the right. I'll be sitting there.

See you soon.

Virginia

Progress Checks

3. d ☐ Ask for information about and find recreational facilities on a map.

What are the people saying?

Do it yourself.

Problem Solving

What's Mickey's problem?

What should Mickey do?
Now role play.

Grammar Summaries

Past Tense of *be* (review)

Was	she it	a student? happy? late
Were	they you	students? happy?

Yes,	she it	was.
	they you	were.

No,	she it	wasn't.
	they you	weren't.

Where	was	he it	yesterday? last Tuesday?
	were	they	
When	was	he	in Mexico?
	were	they	in New York?

He	was	at home.
They	were	

He	wasn't	there in May.
They	weren't	

Simple Past Tense (review)

Did	he she they	take the test?

Yes,	he they	did.

No,	he they	didn't.

When Where	did you he	take the test?

I		took	the test	last week.
You She They	didn't	take		in school.

Should

Should	I he she we	study?

Yes,	you he	should.

No,	you he	shouldn't.

What	should	I she	do?

You She We They	should shouldn't	take the test. study all night.

Future Time with *be going to*

I'm He's She's We're You're They're	(not)	going to	call the dentist. be in today.

Is	he	going to be late?
Are	you	
Am	I	

Yes,	he	is.	No	he	isn't.	(he's not)
	you	are.		you	aren't.	(you're not)
	I	am.				

Where	is	he	going to	go after school?
Why	are	they		be late?

Direct and Indirect Objects

Steve gave a message to	me. you. him. her. us. them.

Steve gave	me a you him her us them	message.

Partitives

some	milk bread chicken

a	carton glass	of milk
	loaf slice	of bread
	package piece	of chicken

Comparisons of Adjectives

big small large cheap	bigger smaller larger cheaper	than

bad good	worse better	than

expensive convenient interesting	more	expensive convenient interesting	than

Past Tense of Irregular Verbs*

break	broke
fall	fell
forget	forgot
get	got
give	gave
go	went
have	had
hurt	hurt
leave	left
meet	met
put	put
see	saw
take	took

(*For a list of irregular verbs, see inside back cover.)

Future Time with *will*

Will	she he it they	be late?

Yes,	she we	will.
No,	he they	won't.

I You He She We They	will	bring it tomorrow.

I You He She We They	will not won't	give it to them.

Superlatives of Adjectives with *-est*

near cheap big thin busy early good bad	the	nearest cheapest biggest thinnest busiest earliest best worst

Verb + Infinitive vs. Modal + Base form of verb

He She	knows how likes	to	work with wood. use power tools.
	can		

Adverbs of Manner

She is	careful. neat. quick. a good worker.

She works	carefully. neatly. quickly. well.

Indefinite Pronouns: *one* and *ones*

Which one?
The blue one or the red one?

Which ones?
The old ones or the new ones?

Future Time with *be* + verb + *ing*

What	is	An Ling	doing	on Monday?
	are	they		
Where	is	she	going	
	are	they		

She's We're	(not)	having a barbecue. going fishing.

Superlatives of Adjectives with *most*

violent interesting boring	the most	violent interesting boring

Past Continuous Tense vs. Simple Past Tense

He	stood	there	for an hour.
	was standing		when he saw the accident.

Possessive Pronouns

Whose	book books	is are	this? these?

It's	her your our my their	book.
They're	his	books.

It's	hers. yours. ours. mine. theirs.
They're	his.

Tapescript

UNIT 1 Page 8 Listening Plus.

Exercise 1. Notice the difference.

Look at the words on the left.

Look at the words on the right. Listen.

Wuh zee your teacher?

Wush she here yesterday?

Exercise 1. Point.

Listen. Point to the words you hear.

Wuh zee in Bridgeton last year?

Wush she at work yesterday?

Wush she at the airport on Sunday?

Wuh zee in your class?

Wush she in Chicago last year?

Wuh zee happy in California?

Exercise 1. Listen and write the sentences.

a. *Wuh zee* a student?

b. *Wush she* at home?

Exercise 2. Point.

Listen to the stories. *Point* to the picture. How do the people feel?

a. Yesterday, Patricia got up at 5:00 a.m. and cooked breakfast for her family. Then she took her children to the babysitter, and she went to work. The work load was very heavy yesterday, and Patricia worked two shifts. At 11:00 p.m., she went home. Patricia was really tired.

b. Erica went to her new ESL class last night. She was late, and she hurried to her seat. Then she looked at the woman sitting at the next desk. She couldn't believe it! She knew her! They were neighborhood friends in the country where she was born. Erica was excited!

c. Last night Ling went to Westside Community Adult School for her first English class. She doesn't understand very much English. She didn't know her teacher, and she didn't know the other students. Ling felt very nervous.

Exercise 2. Write.

Listen to the conversations. How do the characters feel? Write the word under the picture.

1. How does the woman feel?

A: I'm going to my first English class tonight.
B: That's great.
A: Well, I don't know. I don't feel so well.
B: Oh? What's the matter?
A: My knees are shaking, my mouth is dry, and my stomach feels funny.
B: Don't worry, Ling. I know you can do this.

2. How does the woman feel?

A: Hi, Patricia. What's the matter?
B: Nothing much. We were really busy at work last night. Everyone worked double shifts.
A: You worked sixteen hours?
B: Yes, I did.
A: You should go home and get some rest.
B: I think you're right.

3. How does the woman feel?

A: You'll never guess what happened tonight! Do you remember Frau Weiss, our neighbor in Germany?
B: Sure. Why?
A: Well, she's in my English class!
B: Really?
A: Yes! Isn't that wonderful?
B: Let's ask her to come to dinner next week.
A: That's a great idea!

Exercise 3. Fill in the information.

Listen for the last names, dates of birth, and Social Security numbers. Fill in the information on the chart.

a.

A: What's your last name, An Ling?
B: It's Moon, M-O-O-N.
A: M-O-O-N. And when were you born?
B: I was born on April 18, 1954.
A: 4/18/54?
B: That's right.
A: And what's your Social Security number?
B: It's 449-27-2780.
A: 449-27-2780. Thanks.

b.

A: Ilona, how do you spell your last name?
B: It's Varga, V-A-R-G-A.
A: OK, V-A-R-G-A. Is your birthdate 10/3/52?
B: Yes, it is. October 3, 1952.
A: How about your Social Security number?
B: My Social Security number is 170-36-2528.
A: 170-36- . . .?
B: 170-36-2528.

c.

A: Reuben, is this your Social Security number? 322-08-1257?
B: No, it's 322-09-1257.
A: OK, 322-09-1257. And your date of birth?
B: May 3, 1971.
A: 5/3/71. And your last name's Martin, right?
B: No, it's Martinian, M-A-R-T-I-N-I-A-N.
A: M-A-R-T-I-A-N?
B: No. M-A-R-T-I-N-I-A-N.
A: Sorry. Thanks, Reuben. That's all I need.

Exercise 4. What about you?

A : My husband was born in Mexico, I was born in Texas, and our children were born in California. What about you?

UNIT 2 Page 20 Listening Plus.

Exercise 1. Notice the difference.

Look at the words on the left.

Look at the words on the right. Listen.

Dih ja get the notice?

Dih dee study English?

Exercise 1. Point.

Listen. Point to the words you hear.

Dih ja go to the parent-teacher conference?

Dih dee miss school last week?

Dih dee do his homework?

Dih ja phone the teacher?

Dih ja write an absence note?

Dih dee watch TV last night?

Exercise 1. Listen and write the sentences.

a. *Dih dee* take the test?

b. *Dih ja* do the homework?

Exercise 2. Point.

Listen to the stories. Point to the correct picture.

Mohammed has a problem. It's really hard for him to study in his family's small apartment. He has three little brothers, and they like to run and yell and climb on the furniture. Mohammed's uncle lives with them, and he likes to listen to very loud music on the stereo. And then there's the neighbors' dog, who barks when he hears the stereo. Poor Mohammed!

Guadalupe has a problem. Her teacher gives her a lot of homework. She wants to do the homework but she is tired when she comes home. She studies in the bedroom, where it's quiet. She lies down and starts reading, but she always gets sleepy and goes to sleep on the first page.

Exercise 2. Write.

Now listen to the teacher and the parent. What should the students do? Write the teacher's suggestion on the lines under the pictures.

1.

A: Guadalupe is having some problems with reading.
B: She tries to read, but she's tired and she falls asleep before she finishes the lesson.
A: Where does Guadelupe study?
B: In her bedroom. The bedroom is quiet, and she can lie down and be comfortable.
A: Maybe she should study at the kitchen table. Then she won't get sleepy so easily.

2.

A: Mohammed's trying hard in class, but he doesn't always hand in his homework, and his homework assignments are not very good.

B: Yes, homework is a problem for him. We don't have a good place for Mohammed to work. Our apartment is small, and the younger kids are noisy.
A: Maybe Mohammed should study at the library. It's always quiet, and he could concentrate there.
B: That's a good idea. Thanks.

Exercise 3. Fill in the information.

Listen to the information on the school notices. Write the day, date, and time from each notice.

First notice:
A: Please give this notice to all your students. The children will be dismissed at noon on Tuesday, December 21, for the winter break.
B: Excuse me. What time?
A: At 12:00 noon.
B: I'm sorry. Is that Tuesday or Wednesday?
A: Tuesday, December 21, at noon.

Second notice:
A: Did you get this notice from the kids' class?
B: Let's see. Cherie's class is going on a field trip to the museum on Friday morning. You have to sign this permission slip.
C: A field trip? I love field trips! When are we going?
B: Next Friday, March 17.
A: OK, 3/17. What time are they leaving?
B: At 9:00 a.m.
C: Friday morning at 9. Oh, great! No math Friday!

Third notice:
A: George, we got a notice from Hugo's school. There's a Parent-Teacher meeting Wednesday night.
B: This Wednesday? April 5?
A: Yes, April 5. It's at 7:30 in the auditorium.
B: OK. 7:30's no problem for me.

Exercise 4. What about you?

A: I want to learn more English because I want to get a better job and I want to help my children in school. What about you?

UNIT 3 Page 31 Reading and Writing.

Exercise 4. Read the messages.

a. Listen to Tony's telephone conversation with Martha. Read the message on the message form.
A: Good morning. Westside Products.
B: Hi, Martha. It's Tony. Could you please give Mr. Thompson a message for me?
A: Sure.
B: I'm having a lot of problems today, and I'm going to be late. I'll be there as soon as I can.
A: OK. I'll give Mr. Thompson your message.

b. Listen to Mary's conversation with Steve. Read the message on the message form.
A: Hello. Is Reuben there, please? This is Mary Stern, his supervisor at work.
B: No, I'm sorry, he isn't. Can I give him a message?
A: When is he going to be back?
B: I don't know. He's at the dentist.
A: I see. Please ask him to call me.

Exercise 5. Listen. Take a message.

Listen to the telephone conversation. Take a message.

a.
A: Dr. Adkin's office. This is Marion.
B: This is Betty Jones. May I speak to Dr. Adkins?
A: I'm sorry, but the doctor is not in this morning.
B: May I leave a message?
A: Of course.
B: Please ask her to call me at 488-4071. My baby is very sick.
A: OK. I'll give her the message as soon as she comes in.
B: Thanks.

b.
A: Good afternoon. Michael's Restaurant.
B: Hello, Debra. This is Don. I've got a problem.
A: What's the matter?
B: My car has a flat tire, and I have to change it. I'm going to be a little late for work.
A: OK. I'll tell Michael.
B: Thanks, Debra.
A: Sure. Good luck with your tire.

Page 32 Listening Plus.

Exercise 1. Notice the difference.

Look at the words on the left.

Look at the words on the right. Listen.
I'm *gonna* be late.
They *wanna* go.

Exercise 1. Point.

Listen. Point to the words you hear.
I'm *gonna* call the boss.
We *wanna* watch TV.
They *wanna* talk to the teacher.
I'm *gonna* call a tow truck.
She's *gonna* make an appointment.
I *wanna* get a new job.

Exercise 1. Listen and write the sentences.

a. I'm *gonna* go to school.
b. They *wanna* talk to the teacher.

Exercise 2. Point.

Listen to the stories. Point to the correct answer.

1. (busy signal sound)

Marjorie is trying to call her sister, but her sister is always talking on the phone. (busy signal sound) Her phone is always busy. (busy signal sound) Marjorie has called four times, but she always hears a *busy signal.* (busy signal sound)

2.

Wayne picked up the phone and dialed his friend's number. Then he heard this: A strange voice said, "I'm sorry, but the number you have dialed is no longer in service." Maybe his friend has moved and has another phone number.

3. (muzak)

Joyce is going to make an appointment with the dentist. She dials the number, and the receptionist says, "I'm going to put you on hold." Then Joyce hears music on the phone. She listens to the music and waits for the receptionist for a long time. Then the receptionist says, "Thank you for holding. How can I help you?"

4. (dial tone)

Jeff is at a public telephone at the airport. (dial tone) He wants to make a call. He picks up the phone, but he hears a funny tone. (dial tone) Oh, of course, that's just the *dial tone!* (dial tone) Now he's going to put change into the coin slot and make his call.

Exercise 2. Number.

Listen to the conversations. Write the correct number in the box.

Number 1.
A: Paul, can you listen to this? I don't understand this sound on the telephone.
B: Sure, Jacques.
A: I called Henri's Restaurant, but I got some music and a recording. Listen. (The number you have dialed is no longer in service.)

Number 2.
A: What is this? Every time I call Hans, I hear this sound. (busy signal) Is the telephone out of order?
B: No. I think Hans is talking to his girlfriend. Wait an hour and call again.

Number 3.
A: What is this noise on the telephone? I don't understand it.
B: Let me listen. (dial tone) No problem. This sound means you can dial now.
A: Oh. We didn't have the same sound on our telephone in Mexico.

Number 4.
A: This is Terry Smith. I need to change my dental appointment.
B: I'm going to put you on hold for a minute while I check our schedule. (muzak) Sorry to keep you waiting. What can I do for you?

Exercise 3. Fill in the information.

Listen to the recorded messages and write the information on the form.

a. You have reached 983-4000, the offices of Drs. Katz, Binderhoff, and Kline. We're not open now. Please call again during our regular hours, Monday through Friday, 9:00 to 5:00. If this call is an emergency, call us at our emergency number: 866-3215.
b. This is 730-9000. Dr. DiSimone has left for the day. Our hours are 7:00 a.m. to 4:00 p.m., Monday through Friday. Please contact us during these hours. If you have an emergency, you may dial our emergency number, 690-1516.
c. You have dialed 776-1094. Dr. Jamali is not in his office today. Please call again between the hours of 8:00 a.m. and 3:00 p.m., Monday through Thursday. In an emergency, you may call our emergency number, 903-8080.

Exercise 4. What about you?

A: I don't make many long distance calls, but I always call my father on his birthday. What about you?

UNIT 4 Page 44 Listening Plus.

Exercise 1. Notice the difference.

Look at the words on the left.

Look at the words on the right. Listen.
He's having a *cuppa* coffee.
She's ordering a *bowla* soup.

Exercise 1. Point.

Listen. Point to the words you hear.
Peggy is eating a *bowla* cereal.

I'd like a *cuppa* tea.
He ordered a *bowla* chili.
Sam's sipping a *cuppa* hot chocolate.
He has a *cuppa* noodles every day for lunch.
She's put a *bowla* fruit on the table.

Exercise 1. Listen and write the sentences.

a. He's having a *cuppa* soup.
b. She's eating a *bowla* rice.

Exercise 2. Point.

Listen to the announcement. Point to the items on the aisle directory at Best in the West.

Attention shoppers. Don't forget to stop at aisle 6A for our terrific specials. Today only, Frozen Gourmet TV Dinners are $1.00 off the regular price. Stock your home freezer at this low price! And here's something in aisle 6B that you surely don't want to miss: Buy one half-gallon of Daisy Delight Ice Cream at the regular price and get the second half-gallon free! Come on over, ice cream lovers.

Here's a snacker's delight: use your Best in the West coupons to buy Patsy's Potato Chips, a large bag for just 69¢. Yum Yum Tree Chocolate Cookies are $1.59 a box, and Clickity Clackity Crackers are 50¢ off, right now with your Best in the West coupon.

Get ready for those school lunches. Best in the West canned tuna is on special at two cans for a dollar. Need a lunch box beverage? Add some Pure Pleasure Pack-a-Juice, ready for the lunch box and full of vitamins, only $2.39 for six.

Enjoy your shopping at Best in the West. Your satisfaction is our most important commodity.

Exercise 2. Number.

Listen to the shoppers and the customer service clerk. Write the aisle numbers on the aisle directory.

a.

A: Excuse me. Where is the Softee bathroom tissue?
B: Bathroom tissue? It's with the paper products in aisle 2B.
A: Pardon?
B: Aisle 2B, next to the paper towels.
A: Thanks.

b.

A: May I help you?
B: Yes, please. Can you tell me where the canned vegetables are? The ones that are on sale?
A: Sure. They're in aisle 9B, about halfway down.
B: OK. Thanks a lot.

c.

A: I need some help. I can't find the grapefruit juice.
B: Grapefruit juice is with the beverages in aisle 16A.
A: With what? Where?
B: With beverages in aisle 16A.
A: Oh. OK. Thank you.

d.

A: I can't find the Clickety Clackity Crackers. My son only wants Clickety Clackities, and I can't find them anywhere.
B: Crackers are in aisle 14B.
A: 4E?
B: No, 14B. They're on the bottom shelf, near the far end of the aisle.
A: 14B. 14B. Thanks.

Exercise 3. Fill in the information.

Listen to the conversations. People are going to talk about foods. Write the food items on the chart.

a.

A: I'm going to Best in the West, Nancy. Do you need anything?
B: Oh, yes, just a minute. Could you go to the bakery section and get a chocolate cake? I *love* the chocolate cake from Best in the West!
A: Is that all?
B: Let's see. How about some meat? Maybe babyback ribs. I'll make them the way you like them best.
A: OK. What else?
B: A bag of oranges? I forgot to buy fruit yesterday.
A: OK, cake, ribs, and oranges.
B: Oh, wait! And a dozen eggs. Oh, and maybe a container of potato salad from the deli.
A: Whoa! No more, Nancy! Remember the budget!
B: You're right. Thanks, honey.
A: Sure. See you in about an hour.

b.

A: Jeff, what do you want for dinner tonight? I'm going to the supermarket.
B: You know me. I always want steak.
A: Then I suppose you also want a baked potato.
B: That's right. With lots of butter.
A: Uh huh. What should I get for dessert?
B: How about apple pie?
A: With cheese on top?
B: Absolutely! Get a few slices of that really good yellow cheese from the deli.
A: OK. Let me write this down: steak, potatoes, butter, apple pie, and cheese.
B: Hurry back! For some reason, I'm getting *very* hungry!

c.

A: Mom, what are we eating tonight?
B: I don't know, Tim. I'm about to go to the store. Want me to cook hamburgers?
A: Hey, that'd be cool!
B: OK. I'll get some ground beef. Do you want me to get lettuce and tomatoes for your burgers?
A: Lettuce and tomatoes? Sure. And can we get some of those really big hamburger buns from the bakery?
B: Yes, I guess so.
A: And some baked beans from the deli, and some chocolate milk.
B: Anything else, young man?
A: Just one more thing. Can Stan come over for dinner?

Exercise 4. What about you?

A: For dinner I want a piece of chicken, some rice, and a cup of coffee. For dessert, I want a bowl of chocolate ice cream. What about you?

UNIT 5 Page 56 Listening Plus.

Exercise 1. Notice the difference.

Look at the words on the left.

Look at the words on the right. Listen.
I *haftuh* see the doctor.
She *hastuh* get a prescription.

Exercise 1. Point.

Listen. Point to the words you hear.
He *hastuh* change an appointment.
I *haftuh* have some tests.
Rodney *hastuh* quit smoking.
We *haftuh* eat more fruits and vegetables.
Paula *hastuh* get some rest.
You *haftuh* call the babysitter.

Exercise 1. Listen and write the sentences.

a. He *hastuh* stay in bed.
b. I *haftuh* see the doctor.

Exercise 2. Point.

Listen to the conversation. Point to all of Mr. Thompson's *previous health problems*.

A: I need to ask you some questions about your medical history, Mr. Thompson. Your records show that you had an ulcer in 1984. Any stomach trouble now?
B: No, no ulcers. Everything's fine.
A: What about colds? Do you have frequent colds?
B: No, not not this year. Last year I had four or five colds.
A: Your chart also shows that you had tuberculosis when you were a child. Any problems now?
B: No, I'm fine now. And my chest X-rays are always OK.
A: Do you smoke?
B: Yes, but I'm trying hard to stop.
A: Try harder. You can't get a new pair of lungs.
B: I know. You're right...

Exercise 2. Check.

Listen to the conversation. Check Mrs. Tolbert's *previous* and *current* health problems.

A: Mrs. Tolbert, have you had any surgery?
B: Just an appendectomy. I had appendicitis as a child.
A: O.K.... I'm a little worried about your hypertension.
B: I'm sorry, Dr. Denton. You're worried about what?
A: About hypertension. Your blood pressure is too high. Are you taking your medicine?
B: Sometimes I forget. I feel fine.
A: You have heart disease, Mrs. Tolbert. It's very important to take your medicine every day.
B: I'll try my best to remember.

Exercise 3. Fill in the information.

Listen. Fill in the information about the medical appointments.

a.

A: This is Richard Stevenson. I need to make an appointment with Dr. Denton.
B: Why do you need to see the doctor, Mr. Stevenson?
A: I hurt my back at work the week before last, and it still bothers me a lot.
B: Can you come in on Thursday afternoon?
A: Day after tomorrow?
B: Yes, Thursday, May 23. We have an opening at 2:30.
A: 2:30. Yes, that sounds fine.

b.

A: This is Margaret Green. I need to see the doctor right away. It's an emergency.
B: What's the matter, Ms. Green?
A: I have a rash on my face. I look TERRIBLE.
B: When did the rash start?
A: Day before yesterday.
B: Is it painful?
A: No, it doesn't hurt, but it looks TERRIBLE.
B: Can you come in tomorrow, Friday, June 6, at 11:00?
A: I need to come in TODAY. I've got a really important date tonight, and this looks TERRIBLE.
B: I'm sorry, Ms. Green, but tomorrow morning is the earliest opening we have.
A: Oh, no. Maybe I'll just have to break my date.

c.

A: Can I make an appointment to see the doctor?
B: What seems to be the problem?
A: The doctor just needs to check my ulcer.
B: When would you like to come in?
A: How about a week from today?
B: Let's see. That's Wednesday, July 30. How about 10:45?
A: OK. July 30, 10:45.
B: And I need your name.
A: Yes, I guess you do. It's Tyrone King.

Exercise 4. What about you?

A: When I'm sick, I usually go to the clinic, but my friend Marge has a family doctor. What about you?

UNIT 6 Page 68 Listening Plus.

Exercise 1. Notice the difference.

Look at the words on the left.

Look at the words on the right. Listen.
That'll be fine.
It'll cost $5.00.

Exercise 1. Point.

Listen. Point to the words you hear.
That'll be all I need today, Mrs. Pine.
It'll be a little late this afternoon.
That'll be $23.65.
It'll be ready tomorrow at 6:00.
It'll rain tomorrow if I don't take my umbrella.
That'll arrive about 2:30 Tuesday.

Exercise 1. Listen and write the sentences.

a. *That'll* be here at 4:00.
b. *It'll* come on Wednesday.

Exercise 2. Point.

Listen to the descriptions. Point to the correct building.

This was old Mrs. Winfield's home. Now it's four apartments. The tenants like the apartments very much. They are in one of the oldest buldings in Bridgeton, on one of the quietest streets. And the tenants say that the neighbors are the friendliest people in California.

Do you like modern buildings? This new high-rise apartment complex is the newest building in Bridgeton. It has an exercise room, an indoor swimming pool, a beautiful view, and a security guard. It also has the highest rent in town.

Would you prefer a house? This little ranch-style house is perfect for families with young children. The nearest school is just one block away. And the fenced yard is the safest play area you could want.

Exercise 2. Check.

Listen to the conversation. Check *yes* or *no* for the housing.

a.

A: How much is the rent for this apartment?
B: Really cheap for this beauty—only $850.
A: That's a lot of money for a one-bedroom apartment. Are utilities included?
B: Yes, they are. And of course there's a stove and refrigerator, too.
A: How about carpet and drapes?
B: Drapes, yes, but no carpet.
A: OK. How far is it to the nearest bus stop?
B: Really convenient—just a five-minute walk.

b.

A: This looks like a nice little house. Is it furnished?
B: No, but it has a washer and a dryer, as well as a stove and a refrigerator.
A: How about the deposit?
B: The security deposit is one months' rent.
A: And how many bedrooms does it have?
B: It has two large bedrooms, plus a big living room where the children can play.
A: Oh. Only two bedrooms. We really want three.

c.

A: This is really a beautiful apartment. Just look at that view!
B: Yes, very nice. But does it have a dining room? I insist on a dining room.
A: There's covered parking in the basement, and air conditioning, of course.
B: But what about the dining room?
A: The heating system is excellent, there's an elevator, and brand new wall-to-wall carpeting.
B: BUT DOES IT HAVE A DINING ROOM?
A: No.

Exercise 3. Fill in the information.

Listen. Fill in the information about the housing problems.

a.

A: Ms. Rand, this is Rita Morrison. I have a problem in my apartment.
B: What's going on?
A: The sink's leaking and I have water all over the floor.
B: What's your apartment number?
A: Apartment 2G.
B: I'll be there in fifteen minutes.
A: Great.

b.

A: Hi, Ms. Rand. This is Pam in 4G. I don't know what's going on. I've got a real mess here.
B: Yes?
A: The toilet's backing up and leaking all over the bathroom. It's awful.
B: I see.
A: Can you come right now? The carpet in the hall's getting soaked, too.
B: I can't come right now, but I'll be there as soon as I can.
A: Oh, dear. Can you come before 4:00? My mother-in-law's coming for dinner.
B: I'll get there at 4:00. Just hang in there.

c.

A: Ms. Rand, this is Ted Cohen. I called last week about the problem we're having with roaches in the kitchen.
B: Oh, yes.
A: You said you would take care of it, but nothing's happening.
B: Sorry. Everybody's having problems right now.
A: When do you think you can come see about this?
B: I'll come by early next week.
A: Monday?
B: OK, Monday.
A: 7:30?
B: 7:45.

Exercise 4. What about you?

A: My dream house has four bedrooms, a swimming pool, and a big yard. What about yours?

UNIT 7 Page 80 Listening Plus.

Exercise 1. Notice the difference.

Look at the words on the left.

Look at the words on the right. Listen.
I *k'n* work nights.
I *kant* work days.

Exercise 1. Point.

Listen. Point to the word you hear.
I *kant* come tomorrow.
She *k'n* come on Wednesday.
We *kant* work day shift.
I *k'n* work nights.
He *kant* use a power saw.
They *k'n* use a hand saw.

Exercise 1. Listen and write the sentences.

a. They *k'n* come Tuesday.
b. He *kant* work Friday.

Exercise 2. Point.

Listen to the job interview. Look at the job skills in the column on the left. Look at the education and training in the column on the right. Point to the words you hear.

A: Let's talk about your job skills. Can you operate a power sewing machine, Minh Lee?
B: Yes, I can.
A: And can you do basic alterations?
B: Yes.
A: Please tell me something about your education and training. Where did you learn to sew?
B: I learned on the job from my grandmother in Vietnam. She sewed beautifully.
A: I see. Did you study sewing in school?
B: I went to a technical school for one year, to learn power sewing, but I specialize in fine sewing by hand, like my grandmother.
A: I see.

Exercise 2. Check.

Listen to Mr. Ramirez talk about his skills and training. Put a check by the things he says.

A: OK, Mr. Ramirez. Please tell me about your training and what you can do.
B: I graduated from high school in Mexico City, and went to technical school for two years. I learned general office skills there.
A: Can you operate a computer? Do you have any computer training?
B: Yes, I can use a computer. When I came to California, I went to Bridgeton Community College for nine months. I studied English and learned to use a word processor. Here is a letter from my teacher, and here are my school records.

Exercise 3. Fill in the information.

Listen to the conversations. Write the last jobs the people had, the dates for that job, and the wages.

a.
A: Tell me about your last job, please, Charles.
B: I was a cook for Beef 'n' Bottle in Chicago.
A: And how long did you work there?
B: For two years, from June 1989 until August 1991.
A: Really? And what was your pay?
B: In 1991, I was chief cook. I made $15.00 an hour.
A: I see.

b.
A: Please have a seat, Ms. . . . Ramos.
B: Yes, Roberta Ramos.
A: Tell me something about your work experience.
B: I do construction work. I'd like to apply for the carpenter's job you advertised.
A: All right. What was your last job?
B: I was a carpenter for J. C. Smith and Company.
A: And how long did you work for them?
B: Two years. From 1989 to 1991, in Denver.
A: Oh? What were your wages in 1991?
B: I was a head carpenter then, and I made $15.75 an hour.

c.
A: Hello. I'm Willis Slocumb. I called earlier. Do you still have a job opening for a day care worker?
B: Yes, we do. But we only hire people with experience and references.
A: Sure. I worked in a day care center in Minnesota for two and a half years. References are no problem.
B: And when did you work there?
A: From 1990 until 1992.
B: How much were you earning then?
A: The pay wasn't so good—$5.25 an hour—but the kids were great. I really enjoyed that job.
B: Then why did you leave?
A: My wife didn't like the cold weather in Minnesota, so we moved here to Hawaii last month.
B: Hmmmmmm.

Exercise 4. What about you?

A: I like to help people. Next year I want to get a job in a hospital. In ten years I want to be a nurse. What about you?

UNIT 8 Page 92 Listening Plus.

Exercise 1. Notice the difference.

Look at the words on the left.

Look at the words on the right. Listen.
Giv'im the hammer.
I *met'er* yesterday.

Exercise 1. Point.

Listen. Point to the words you hear.
Hey ! *Giv'im* the scissors!
I *told'er* the whole story.
Wait! *Tell'er* the address!
Emily *handed 'im* the stamps.
Miss Jones *gave 'er* the correct change.
Dad! *Tell 'im* the news!

Exercise 1. Listen and write the sentences.

a. *Giv'im* the address.
b. Jane *met'er* at the supermarket.

Exercise 2. Point.

Listen to the descriptions. Look at the pictures. Point to the correct one.

a. Point to the things on the desk. This is Fred's desk at the hotel. Fred has two telephones. The telephone on the left, the black one, is the house phone. The white telephone, the one on the right, is for outside calls.
Fred also has two staplers on his desk. The large stapler, the one next to the black telephone, is for stapling 20 pages or more. Fred uses the small stapler, the one on the right, for stapling short messages.

b. Point to the things on the shelves. This is the storeroom in the hotel. There are four boxes of envelopes on the shelves. The small boxes, the ones on the left, contain envelopes for keys. The ones on the right, the large boxes, contain envelopes for receipts.
There are also two kinds of cleaner on the shelves. The housekeepers use the bottles of window cleaner, the ones on the bottom shelves, for mirrors. They use the cans of cleaner on the top shelves for furniture.

Exercise 2. Circle.

Listen to the conversations. Circle the correct items in the picture.

a.
A: Tom, please take a stapler to Roy in the office.
B: Okay. Which one does he want, the large one or the small one?
A: Take the (mumble, mumble)
B: I'm sorry. Which one?
A: The large one, the one next to the telephone. I need the other one right now.
B: OK. I'll do it right away.

A: I'm having trouble with this telephone. I can't get a dial tone.
B: You have two telephones here. Which one is it that doesn't work?
A: It's the new one, the white one.
B: Well, let's see what's wrong.

b.
A: What do you want me to do now, Mrs. Hill?
B: Ms. Mathers needs a box of envelopes. They're in the storeroom on the bottom shelf.
A: Which envelopes does she want, the small ones or the large ones?
B: The large ones.

A: I don't like this window cleaner. It leaves streaks on the mirrors.
B: Really? Which one is that?
A: The aerosol.
B: Which one? The one on the top shelf?
A: Yes.

Exercise 3. Fill in the information.

Listen to the conversations. Write the jobs the people are doing and the problems they have.

a.
A: Henry, can you help me?
B: Sure, Marie. What's the problem?
A: I need to make some copies, but the copy machine is jammed.
B: Hmmm. Yes, it is. Take these papers out and push the reset button.
A: The reset button? Which one is that?
B: This red one right here.
A: Okay, it's fine now. Thanks a lot, Henry.
B: Sure. Any time.

b.
A: Please clean room 102, Oscar.
B: Can't do it. The vacuum cleaner is making a strange noise.
A: Hmm. I think you need a new bag. Just use the other vacuum for now.
B: Oh.

c.
A: I want to use the computer for these letters, but it isn't working.
B: Let me see it, Rosalie. What's wrong?
A: I press the switch, but nothing happens.
B: Oh. You just forgot to plug it in.
A: You're right! Silly me!

Exercise 4. What about you?

A: I like to work with other people, but my friend likes to work alone. What about you?

UNIT 9 Page 104 Listening Plus.

Exercise 1. Notice the difference.

Look at the words on the left.

Look at the words on the right. Listen.
Whaddya doing?
Where're ya going?

Exercise 1. Point.

Listen. Point to the words you hear.
Whaddya watching?
Where're ya playing football?
Where're ya going bowling?
Whaddya doing this afternoon?
Where're ya studying tonight?
Whaddya thinking about?

Exercise 1. Listen and write the sentences.

a. *Where're ya* going fishing?
b. *Whaddaya* doing tonight?

Exercise 2. Point.

Look at the picture. Point to the activities you hear.

One of the things Marie likes to do on Saturday evenings is have dinner with her boyfriend. He's a wonderful cook and he often cooks for the two of them.

Kim likes a lot of sports, but her favorite sport is volleyball. Kim is a very good player. She plays for the Lucky Seven team. They play every Thursday evening. Right now, Kim's team is number one in its league.

When Joji and Yuki have free time, they go to the movies. They like almost every kind of movie, but Yuki's favorite movies are funny, and Joji's are thrillers.

Reading is Heidi's favorite thing to do. Whenever she has any free time, she goes to the library and checks out a book. She likes lots of books, but she especially likes mystery books.

Exercise 2. Number.

Listen to the conversations. Write the correct number in the box.

Number 1.

A: Did you like it?
B: Yeah, I thought it was great!
A: Really? I thought it was the most violent movie I've ever seen! It gave me a terrible headache.
B: That's too bad. You can pick the movie next time.

Number 2.

A: Oooh, don't turn off the light!
B: Why not?
A: This short story is really scary!
B: What are you reading?
A: "The Pit and the Pendulum" by Edgar Allen Poe.
B: Oh, right! I read that story.
A: It's absolutely the most frightening story I've ever read.

Number 3.

A: Did you win?
B: Of course! No, seriously, we did win, but the score was really close.
A: Was it a good game?
B: Yes, it was. It was the most exciting game we've had all season.

Number 4.

A: What did you do last night?
B: I had the most romantic evening I've ever had.
A: Did you go out to dinner with your boyfriend?
B: No. He cooked a wonderful French meal and we had dinner by candlelight.
A: It sounds just like a fairy tale.

Exercise 3. Fill in the information.

Listen to the conversations and write the weather information.

a.

A: Here's your ticket. You're booked on Flight 162 to New York LaGuardia on March 16.
B: What's the weather like in New York then? What clothes should I pack?
A: March in New York is cool and rainy. Be sure to take an umbrella.

b.

A: Now here's the weather for the Bridgeton area on this Fourth of July weekend. We can expect warm, sunny days, great weather for going to the lake.

c.

A: Hi, Mom. I got my plane ticket for Denver, and I'm all set.
B: That's great, Meg. When will you be here?
A: My flight gets to Denver on Tuesday, July 2. What'll the weather be like there?
B: It's supposed to be just beautiful, hot and sunny.
A: Good. I'll bring my swim suit.

d.

A: Look, Fred. Here's an article on Bridgeton, where Janice and Roy live!
B: Is that so? Well, what does it say?
A: It's about their weather this December. Let's see. It says it's cool, and they're having a lot of rainy weather. Roy will be glad about that.
B: Guess so. I don't like rainy weather, myself.

e.

A: Here's a winter weather advisory for Denver and the metropolitan area for tomorrow, December 2. We can expect very cold weather, with snow. Snow tires or chains are required on the mountain passes. Drive carefully.

f.

A: This New York weather is wearing me out!
B: Yeah. July is always SO HOT! I don't want to do anything.
A: I wish we could go swimming.
B: Me, too, but it's going to be stormy this afternoon.
A: Again? Yuck.

g.

A: You're going to love Bridgeton's weather forecast for today. For this Friday, March 5, we'll have a beautiful warm day, with lots of sun. It will be a perfect day to work in the garden.

h.

A: Just look at that rain! Denver's going to wash away.
B: That's what you say about Denver every March, Alice, and it hasn't washed away yet.
A: Well, I guess this rainy weather is OK—if you're a duck.

i.

A: I've got to take Ritchie to the specialist on December 15.
B: To New York?
A: Yes. I don't really like to fly into the city in winter.
B: It will probably be cold and cloudy tomorrow. I hope you have a safe trip.

Exercise 4. What about you?

A: My favorite holiday in the U.S. is Thanksgiving, because I love turkey! What about you?

UNIT 10 Page 116 Listening Plus.

Exercise 1. Notice the difference.

Look at the words on the left.

Look at the words on the right. Listen.
Why'er ya late?
Where wer ya going?

Exercise 1. Point.

Listen. Point to the words you hear.
Why'er ya working on Sunday?
Where were ya last night when I called?
Where were ya skiing yesterday?
Why'er ya wearing my shirt?
Where were ya when the storm started?
Why'er ya asking all these questions?

Exercise 1. Listen and write the sentences.

a. *Where were ya* going to school last year?
b. *Why'er ya* taking this class?

Exercise 2. Point.

Look at the picture of the accident. Three people saw the accident. Point to the witness who's being described.

When the accident happened, Fritz was on Arizona Street. He was on his motorcycle, and he was waiting for the light to turn green at the intersection of Arizona and 8th Avenue. He saw the crash very clearly.

Phyllis was on 8th Avenue at the intersection of 8th Avenue and Arizona Street when the accident occurred. She was on roller skates, and she was going north on 8th Avenue. She was very near the accident site.

Juan was waiting for his bus. He was standing at the bus stop on Arizona Street, at the southwest corner of the intersection. He was reading a newspaper, but he looked up just before the accident, and witnessed the whole thing.

Exercise 2. Number.

Listen to the conversations. Each of the people believe someone (or something) different caused the accident. Write the number 1 by the person or thing Fritz names.

Number 1.

A: Now please tell me exactly what you saw.
B: Well, like I said, I was on my bike going west on Arizona Street. The truck driver was heading east on Arizona, and the driver of the car was heading south on 8th Avenue.
A: Yes. Now what happened?
B: The truck driver wasn't paying any attention to his driving. He was talking to his friend when the accident happened!
A: OK. Truck driver was talking to a friend.
B: And he ran right through the red light and hit the car! The truck driver was definitely wrong.
A: Are you sure about that? The truck ran the red light?
B: I'm positive, officer.
A: I see.

Write the number 2 by the person or thing Phyllis names.

Number 2.

A: I'm really shaky! That was terrible!
B: You saw the accident?
A: Oh, yes, I did! I saw the whole thing!
B: What did you see?
A: Oh, I don't know! I'm so nervous that I can't even think!
B: Just take your time.
A: Well, the truck driver was just a hero! A real hero!
B: What do you mean by that, ma'am?
A: Well, a little black dog—the cutest little thing you ever saw—ran right in front of the truck. The truck driver was just wonderful! He swerved just in time, and the little dog was safe!
B: But the truck driver hit the car.

A: That's right, but nobody was hurt, and the little dog is okay.
B: You think the dog caused the accident?
A: Oh, yes. Definitely. It was the dog's fault. But he didn't *mean* to, you know.

Write the number 3 by the person or thing Juan names.

Number 3.
A: I believe the driver of the car was completely in the wrong, Officer.
B: Why do you say that?
A: The light was definitely red, and she didn't slow down at all. In fact, she went *faster*. There's no doubt about it.
B: So the driver of the car caused the accident?
A: Absolutely. She was entirely to blame.

Exercise 3. Fill in the information.

Listen to the conversations and write *where to catch the bus, where to get off the bus,* and *what time to catch the bus.*

a. Kenji is asking for bus information.
A: Bridgeton Busways. Can you hold, please?
B: OK.
A: Sorry to keep you waiting.
B: I need route information, please.
A: Where are you right now, sir? What are the cross streets?
B: I'm on Lincoln between Tenth and Eleventh Avenues.
A: And where do you want to go?
B: To Kansas and Valley Highway.
A: And what time do you need to get there?
B: By 7:30 a.m.
A: OK, that's Route A. You catch the Valley bus at Lincoln and Eighth Avenue at 6:44.
B: Excuse me. Could you repeat that?
A: Yes. Go to the bus stop at Lincoln and Eighth Avenue. Catch the 6:44 bus.
B: OK. Lincoln and Eighth at 6:44. Do I need a transfer?
A: No, you don't. That bus will take you right to Kansas and Valley.
B: And what's the fare?
A: 75¢. And you must have the exact change.
B: Thanks.

b. Yolanda wants to meet her friend Tom at Bridgeton Drive. They're going to the mountains for a picnic.
A: I need some information about your bus service to Bridgeton Drive and Washington Street.
B: What is your location, please?
A: I'm sorry. What?
B: Where are you right now?
A: Let's see. I'm on Delaware between Fifth and Sixth.
B: OK. That's Route B. You need to catch the bus at the bus stop at Delaware and Fifth. And what's your destination?
A: I want to go to Bridgeton Drive and Washington.
B: Take the bus to the King Street bus station. Then get off the bus and walk west a couple of blocks to Bridgeton and Washington.
A: Is this right? I catch the bus at Delaware and Fifth and I get off at King Street?
B: That's right.
A: I need to be there at 8:00 tomorrow morning.
B: OK. You can catch the 7:33 bus.
A: Route B, 7:33, corner of Delaware and Fifth.
B: Perfect!

c. Binh is going to his sponsor's house for dinner.
A: This is BUS-INFO, 287-4636. How may I help you?
B: I need some information, please. I live on Second Avenue and Main Street.
A: And where do you want to go, sir?
B: To Arizona Street, near Valley Highway.
A: Let's see. You're going to need to transfer . . . OK. You should catch the bus going south at Second Avenue and Arizona Street.
B: Excuse me. Please speak slowly.
A: OK. Start at Second Avenue and Arizona.
B: Start at Second Avenue and Arizona.
A: That's right. Then you need to transfer to the northbound bus at Eighth Avenue and Delaware Street.
B: OK.
A: The Kansas Street bus will take you right to Arizona and Valley.
B: Good. I want to get there at 6:30 p.m.
A: Then you need to depart at 5:48.
B: Pardon me. What time?
A: Take the bus that leaves at 5:48. That's 12 minutes before 6:00.
B: OK. Thank you very much.
A: Thank you for calling Bridgeton Busways.

Exercise 4. What about you?

A: When I go on a long trip, I don't like to drive. I like to ride on the bus and see everything. What about you?

Basic Conversations

for Progress Checks: *What are the people saying?*

(These are suggested answers. Students' answers will vary.)

Unit 1

2. A: Hi, (name). It's good to see you.
   B: Hi, (name). How are you doing?
   A: Fine, thanks.

   A: (Name), this is (name).
   B: Glad to meet you, (name).
   C: Nice to meet you, too.

   A: See you soon.
   B: So long.
   C: Goodbye.

3. A: Where are you from?
   B: I'm from South Korea.
   A: When did you come to the United States?
   B: I came here in 1985.

   A: How did you feel when you came to the United States?
   B: I was very happy and excited to see my family and friends.

Unit 2

3. A: Excuse me. Which way is the ladies' room?
   B: Go down the hall. It's the third door on the left.
   A: Thanks.

5. A: What should my daughter do?
   B: Maybe she should study in a quiet place.

Unit 3

1. A: Hello, Mary?
   B: I think you have the wrong number.
   A: Oh, I'm sorry.

4. A: Directory assistance. What city please?
   B: Bridgeton. May I have the number for Clark Dooley at 100 South Broadway?
   A: Hold on, please. That's 235-7602.

Unit 4

3. A: I bought this package of chicken yesterday and it's bad. Here's my receipt.
   B: I'm sorry. Do you want another package?
   A: Yes, please. OR No, thanks. I'd like a refund/my money back, please.

Unit 5

2. A: Hello, this is (name). I'd like to make an appointment to see the doctor.
   B: Why do you need to see the doctor?
   A: I have a pain in my stomach.
   B: Can you come in at 2:30 tomorrow?
   A: Sure. Tomorrow is fine. Thank you.

3. A: Hello, this is (name). I called this morning. I have to change my appointment.
   B: OK. When was your appointment?
   A: On Tuesday at 10:00.
   B: And when do you want to come in?
   A: How about Wednesday?
   B: OK. How's Wednesday at 9:30?
   A: That's fine. Thank you.

Unit 6

2. A: Are two people OK?
   B: Well, yes, but no more than two people.
   A: When will the apartment be available?
   B: It will be available November 1st. When will you bring in the security deposit?
   A: I'll bring it in on Friday.

   A: Where's the nearest bus stop?
   B: It's on Park and 21st and the nearest school is at Lincoln and 23rd.

4. A: May I help you?
   B: What are the start-up costs for gas service and electric service, please?
   A: We'll need a $20 deposit. And you'll have to pay an installation fee of $10.
   B: OK.
   A: What's your new address?
   B: It's 222 First Avenue, Apartment 5B.
   A: When do you want service to start?
   B: We're moving in on the first.
   A: Fine. We'll send a representative between 8:00 and 1:00 on the first.
   B: Thank you.

Unit 7

2. A: Mr. (name). I'm (name).
   B: How do you do? Please have a seat.
   A: Thank you.
   B: What job are you interested in?
   A: I'm looking for a job as a gardener.

B: Do you have any experience? What are your skills?
A: I was a gardener in Mexico for two years, from 1989 to 1990. I can use power machines and I know how to care for flowers.
B: Where did you get your training?
A: I worked in my uncle's business. I learned on the job.
B: Where did you go to school?
A: I went to high school in Mexico and adult school here in Bridgeton.
B: Very good. Why should my company hire you, Ms. (name)? What are your strengths?
A: Well, I'm never late and I work very carefully.
B: Thank you very much, Ms. (name). We'll call you.
A: Thank you, Mr. (name).

Unit 8

4. A: Your work is too slow.
   B: I'm sorry. I'll try to work faster.

   A: (Male name), I have a problem. This vacuum cleaner is making a strange noise.
   B: Let me see. Maybe I can fix it.

Unit 9

2. A: What's the weather forecast?
   B: It will be warm and sunny.
   A: What are you doing this weekend?
   B: I'm playing volleyball on Saturday. On Sunday we're having a barbecue. What about you?
   A: I'm going to the movies on Saturday night. And on Sunday, I'm going fishing.

3. A: What's your favorite American holiday?
   B: New Year's.
   A: What do you usually do on New Year's Eve?
   B: We have a party.
   A: How do you celebrate New Year's Eve in your country?
   B: *(Answers will vary.)*

Unit 10

3. A: Where's a good place to camp?
   B: Blue River.
   A: Thanks. And where's a good place to fish?
   B: Green Lake. It's near Blue River.